Ask, Listen, Empower

MARY DAVIS FOURNIER is the deputy director of the American Library Association's Public Programs Office, where she specializes in institutional partnerships, scaling impact, and new project development for all types of libraries. Fournier has spearheaded dozens of groundbreaking initiatives that have paved the way for innovation in the field, including Libraries Transforming Communities and the National Impact of Library Public Programs Assessment (NILPPA). She has an MEd in education policy studies from the University of Illinois at Urbana–Champaign and a BA in history and English literature from the University of Wisconsin–Madison.

SARAH OSTMAN is the communications manager for the American Library Association's Public Programs Office, where she serves as editor of ProgrammingLibrarian.org, a web resource for library professionals, and oversees communications for national library programming initiatives including Libraries Transforming Communities. Before joining ALA and the library field in 2014, she spent nearly a decade as a newspaper reporter, editor, and freelance writer. Sarah has an MA in journalism from Columbia College Chicago and a BA in sociology and theater from Smith College.

ISBNs
978-0-8389-4740-1 (paper)
978-0-8389-4834-7 (PDF)
978-0-8389-4832-3 (ePub)
978-0-8389-4833-0 (Kindle)

Library of Congress Cataloging-in-Publication Data
Names: Fournier, Mary Davis, editor. | Ostman, Sarah, editor.
Title: Ask, listen, empower : grounding your library work in community engagement / edited by Mary Davis Fournier and Sarah Ostman ; foreword by Tracie D. Hall.
Description: Chicago : ALA Editions, 2021. | "ALA Public Programs Office." | Includes bibliographical references and index. | Summary: "This important resource provides targeted guidance on how libraries can effectively engage with the public to address a range of issues for the betterment of their community, whether it is a city, neighborhood, campus, or something else"—Provided by publisher.
Identifiers: LCCN 2020028180 (print) | LCCN 2020028181 (ebook) | ISBN 9780838947401 (paperback) | ISBN 9780838948323 (epub) | ISBN 9780838948347 (pdf) | ISBN 9780838948330 (kindle edition)
Subjects: LCSH: Libraries and community—United States. | Libraries and Society—United States.
Classification: LCC Z716.4 .A84 2021 (print) | LCC Z716.4 (ebook) | DDC 021.20973—dc23
LC record available at https://lccn.loc.gov/2020028180
LC ebook record available at https://lccn.loc.gov/2020028181

Composition by Alejandra Diaz in the Questa and Sofia typefaces. Cover design by Karen Sheets de Gracia.

♾ This paper meets the requirements of ANSI/NISO Z39.48-1992 (Permanence of Paper).

Printed in the United States of America
25   24   23   22   21   5   4   3   2   1

CONTENTS

FOREWORD

TRACIE D. HALL

In the early 2000s, fresh out of library school, I was hired to run the Albany Branch of the Hartford (Connecticut) Public Library (HPL), located in a culturally rich but economically disinvested community, predominantly inhabited by Black and brown residents, many of them from the Caribbean. Like many institutions serving under-resourced communities, the library worked earnestly to meet the traditional library and layered informatics needs of its constituency despite a limited materials budget, too few staff (we were adjacent to a middle school and within four blocks of both an elementary and a high school), and a building with an aged façade and interior in immediate need of renovation. Children packed the library after school in numbers too overwhelming to facilitate the kind of after-school homework help and programming they deserved. Adults, having long since ceded the library to the children, underutilized it, resulting in its perennially having among the lowest circulation numbers in the system. Rather than the branch being a true asset to the community, the library's service gaps unintentionally underscored its needs.

It would take the leadership of former Hartford Public Library Chief Louise Blalock (recognized in 2001 as *Library Journal*'s Librarian of the Year) and HPL managers like Anwar Ahmad to shake things up and turn things around. They did this mainly by being willing to take risks. One of those risks was on me. I came onto the job with my newly minted MLIS from the University of Washington's Information School. Though by then I'd worked a few years in program roles at the Seattle Public Library and the New Haven Free Public Library, I still leaned heavily on my social work background from my early career days as the director of a youth homeless shelter. I'd focused on youth services in my library work and had taken on projects supporting library services for homeless families and children and those living in public housing, youth in foster care, and career development for adults with low literacy. Under Blalock and Ahmad's stewardship, HPL had retired the title "branch librarian" in favor of "community librarian." When he recruited and hired me, Ahmad advised that my monthly report should show that my work was being felt as much in the neighborhood as it was within the branch's four walls.

Inspired by this proactive model of librarianship in which we were expected to anticipate and not just respond to residents' needs, I worked to become a more effective advocate for my community—someone to rally support for their interests and bring attention to their strengths as well as their struggles. I lobbied for resources to improve the appearance and function of the library, created early literacy programs for Head Start and day-care facilities and adult literacy courses, offered multilevel computer classes, and produced cultural programs that reflected the diverse makeup of our residents.

And importantly, I joined and encouraged my staff to join school and community organizations and advisory boards, which helped increase the community's familiarity with the library. Residents saw that the Albany Branch had skin in the game, that we cared—that we were invested in the future of the entire community and its residents, not just what happened in the building.

Slowly but surely things started to change. Circulation went up, program attendance—importantly, by adults—climbed. The look and feel of the branch changed, and we became a point of pride. I remember one of our regular users walking in with a companion and standing in the middle of the floor as they both looked around. When I came over to ask if I could be of assistance, he smiled and answered, "No, Ms. Hall. This is my cousin. I just wanted him to see our library."

Our library—that deeply felt sense of collective ownership is what we had been working for. Sometime after, the *Hartford Courant* would profile the branch's turnaround in an article it titled "A Light Shines on Albany Avenue." A year or so later, when I announced that I was leaving Hartford to lead ALA's Office for Diversity, one of our most devoted library users told me that I had brought a sense of energy to the library that had changed his expectations of what a library could be. It remains one of the greatest compliments I've ever received.

This is the power of libraries. We are more than buildings full of books and computers. We are essential resources in the fight for information equity, yes. But we are also inherently democratic places for conversation, connection, and exchange. We are gateways to all the information in the world, places where the richest and poorest, the most regarded and the most disregarded among us may access the same resources for the same cost: nothing at all. We offer infinite possibilities on equal footing, and so we offer hope and opportunity.

It is incumbent upon librarians to maintain this equal footing. It's our job to ensure that all users have access to an array of arguments, sometimes competing arguments, so they can make their own decisions about the world and their place in it. Often—especially today, in our increasingly siloed, echo-chambered society—that means libraries must curate and host the conversations themselves.

The voices in this book speak of libraries that are breaking down the walls that separate them from their communities, libraries that are helping to ensure that their communities are seen and heard. The process isn't easy, and it may not come naturally to all of us. Community engagement asks us not only to interact with the people we serve but to understand, empathize with, and build systems of service that respond to their needs and concerns.

The effort to make good on librarianship's greatest goal—to forge a world that invites our communities to learn, grow, and improve—cannot be done behind a reference desk or around a conference table. It requires legwork and embeddedness, partnership and shared power. Libraries have the potential and, I would argue, unique positionality to help our communities realize their highest and most just visions of themselves. That is the work: to empower our communities, to take on their dreams and challenges, to be a partner and modeler in not only setting the table in an information-centered society but also constructing enough chairs to make sure everyone—especially those most likely to be left out—gets a seat. It's a big ask, I know, but libraries can do it. Libraries must do it. And as the pages of this book show, we already are.

ACKNOWLEDGMENTS

This book would not have been possible without the work of numerous individuals and organizations that have supported both the American Library Association (ALA) and the wider library field as they have embraced community engagement as a foundational part of librarianship. Thank you to past ALA Presidents Maureen Sullivan, Barbara Stripling, Courtney Young, and Nancy Kranich and ALA executive directors Tracie Hall, Mary Ghikas, and Keith Michael Fiels for their visionary leadership, and to Susan Hildreth, Deborah Jacobs, and Jessica Dorr for their generosity as thought partners and leaders in innovative funding. Thanks to the National Coalition for Dialogue and Deliberation (NCDD), the Chief Officers of State Library Agencies (COSLA), the Association for Rural and Small Libraries (ARSL), the Harwood Institute for Public Innovation, and the team at Knology for their collaboration throughout the ongoing implementation of ALA's Libraries Transforming Communities initiative, and to the Bill & Melinda Gates Foundation and the Institute of Museum and Library Services (IMLS), especially program officers Sarah Fuller and Sandra Toro, for their critical support of this work. And gratitude to our colleagues at the American Library Association, our partners at the Public Library Association and the Association of College and Research Libraries, our editor, Jamie Santoro, and especially Deb Robertson and the rest of our peers in the ALA Public Programs Office. Collectively this group has made visible the rising tide of library-led community engagement throughout the United States.

INTRODUCTION

MARY DAVIS FOURNIER

If I were permitted to select one term to capture the paradigm of librarianship in these times it would be *community engagement*. The term is ubiquitous these days and often confused with marketing, programming, outreach, and advocacy. Although it may include all those things, community engagement is an active dynamic all its own.

What is community engagement, exactly? Practitioners across the field helped us to arrive at this definition: community engagement is the process of working collaboratively with community members—be they library users, residents, faculty, students, or partner organizations—to address issues for the betterment of the community.

Some in the library field remain dubious about the need for a new understanding of the phrase. Ask a career librarian and that person may reason that the library is, by definition, engaged with its community; for a library to exist, it must provide something that the individuals in its community use and want and need. Some library workers marvel at new job titles like "community engagement librarian" and wonder, "Isn't that what we've been doing all along?"

The answer is a resounding yes. But libraries and library workers are practicing community engagement in new and different ways, with focus on building community, accessing skills that respond to our age's love-hate relationship with technology, isolation, media, collective impact, and communication. Through the practice of community engagement, libraries are doing the work they always have done but are working to fill gaps that may not have fallen to libraries before, and they are adapting to do it better. One needs to look back no farther than the COVID-19 global pandemic to see community engagement innovation at its finest: librarians reaching out to their patrons through accelerated use of social media and web resources, as well as old-fashioned telephone calls and even library window displays to engage and inform service during a time of mandated isolation. However, the rapid pivot from in-person to online delivery also pointed to the severity of the digital divide and showed how easily people can still be left behind. These challenges have tested libraries' approaches to community engagement and revealed how much work we still need to do to fulfill our profession's commitment to community collaboration, empowerment, and equitable access to information.

As Nancy Kranich explores in our first chapter, U.S. libraries are anchored in the traditions and ideals of civic engagement. So perhaps it should not come as a surprise that the COVID-19 pandemic challenged libraries to amplify these ideals, just as the Great Recession of 2007 thrust many libraries farther to the forefront of community impact. In some of the harder-hit communities, school, public, and college libraries found themselves among the only institutions with the combination of community expertise and culture of responsiveness to help. "The importance of libraries in American life continued to grow in 2008—and accelerated dramatically as the national economy sank and people looked for sources of free, effective help in a time of crisis," notes ALA's 2009 *State of America's Libraries* report. Even as budgets were slashed, libraries acted as community hubs for job seekers and others hit hardest by the collapse.

About this time, from my vantage point in ALA's Public Programs Office, I began to witness library practitioners creating opportunities for dialogue and conversation that went beyond traditional book and film discussions—they led conversations about the importance of community, civility, and compassion; spoke about the complexities of race and equity; and invited the public in for frank discussions of library funding. (Later, we would see heroic responses from libraries like the Ferguson Public Library in Missouri, which served as a community gathering place in the unrest after a police officer shot and killed Michael Brown in 2014.) Libraries began reaching out to me and my ALA colleagues for help navigating these conversations. The Public Programs Office began to explore the impact of dialogue-driven library work with support from organizations like the Fetzer Institute, the Bill & Melinda Gates Foundation, and the National Endowment for the Humanities to learn just what libraries would do with the opportunity to create dialogue-to-action programs that responded to community issues.

In response, ALA's community engagement initiative, Libraries Transforming Communities, was born. Since 2014, ALA has offered free training, grant opportunities, and resources to encourage libraries on this journey. We began by collaborating with the Harwood Institute for Public Innovation and later joined with the National Coalition for Dialogue and Deliberation and others. In the process, thousands of libraries around the world—from the United States to India to New Zealand—have learned from and used our materials to better understand their users and nonusers, to lead conversations on hot-button issues, and to move from dialogue to action. And though there have been achievements in the form of political action, retooled programs, approved library tax levies, and increased library leverage, the most significant successes have been countless small events with respectful listening and learning by people across the country. It is these events, in and outside the library, fostered and often led by library workers, that are shifting the field, libraries as institutions, and library practitioners to fully occupy their roles as the "palaces of the people" in this century.

And ALA has not been the only actor in supporting this expansion of the library's role. A convergence of activity and innovation in the realm of needs assessment and program impact in the field led by the Public Library Association (PLA), the Association of College and Research Libraries (ACRL), the Chief Officers of State Library Agencies (COSLA), OCLC, and the Urban Libraries Council, and amplified by the work of the Aspen Institute, the Pew Research Center, the Institute of Museum and Library Services, and others, has positioned the field to navigate these seemingly endless waves of societal transition.

In these pages, we will peek into the world of library-led community engagement from a variety of angles, from the theoretical to the pragmatic. Kranich, for decades one of the foremost leaders in library-led community engagement, will take us through the unique foundation of civic engagement laid by U.S. libraries throughout the past centuries. Erica Freudenberger and Susan Hildreth explore how libraries can—and do—use their social capital to empower people to enact agency in their lives and communities and make the change they want to see in the world. Hadiya Evans describes how her Denver Public Library created a unique reading and discussion series in response to the community's turmoil over the killings of African Americans at the hands of police. Cindy Fesemyer shares her delightfully practical approach to partnership building, one of the foundations of community work. And that is only our first few chapters.

This book is intended to examine the context, implications, and applications of library community engagement today. It is meant to be a book for present and future library workers, for lifelong learners within the profession, and, perhaps, for the many collaborators in the work of libraries. We hope to acknowledge and amplify the experiences, lessons learned, pathways to success, and expanding models for library-led community engagement. Although this book is by no means exhaustive, the contributors each exemplify the realized potential for this work and provide valuable insight, perspectives, and wisdom to get you started, whether you are an MLIS student, a mid-career professional, or just starting out in the world of libraries.

DEMOCRACY, COMMUNITY, AND LIBRARIES

NANCY KRANICH

A t the turn of the twenty-first century, political scientist Robert Putnam reported that Americans were "bowling alone"—leading lives increasingly disconnected from each other and the institutions of civic life. "For the first two-thirds of the twentieth century a powerful tide bore Americans into ever deeper engagement in the life of their communities, but a few decades ago—silently, without warning—that tide reversed and we were overtaken by a treacherous rip current," Putnam wrote. "Without at first noticing, we have been pulled apart from one another and from our communities over the last third of the century."[1]

Putnam observed lower rates of voting, curtailed work with political parties and service organizations, fewer people joining civic groups, and lower attendance at community meetings and political events. A series of forums convened to examine challenges to democracy revealed that participants felt they were bystanders instead of active members of our democracy—consumers rather than citizen proprietors. Others saw themselves as local but not national participants—like citizens of city-states rather than a national democracy. Forum participants also expressed concern about the loss of public space where citizens might meet informally to discuss community problems and political issues in a civil manner. In short, they saw the average citizen as unrepresented, voiceless, and homeless.[2] These sentiments were corroborated by a 2019 Pew Research Center poll that found that 85 percent of Americans are more negative about political discourse in the United States, prompting further withdrawal from the public sphere.[3] Moreover, Americans have lost confidence in our national institutions, as reflected in another Pew poll that found that only 18 percent of Americans trust the government in Washington to do what's right "just about always" or "most of the time," a drastic decrease from even fifteen years ago.[4]

Even as people lose trust in our national government, they continue to hold high opinions of their state and local governments, feeling local government is more responsive and less partisan. A 2018 Pew poll found that 67 percent of Americans had a "very" or "mostly" favorable view of their local government, compared to just 35 percent with a favorable view of the federal government.[5] Numerous other studies have shown that neighborliness and civic life are not dead but flourishing in some locales—so much so that it brings with it a sense of opportunity, possibility, and even optimism. Many Americans continue to believe that increased public engagement can rejuvenate hope and the public-mindedness that typify this nation at its best. If they are to fulfill their role as citizen proprietors—a role that prompts them to own shared problems as "ours" and not "theirs"—they want a greater sense of community, safer public spaces, and increased trust.[6] At a time when gaps are widening between citizens across the country, they turn to catalytic, boundary-spanning institutions in their local communities to provide a safe (and brave) place for them to exercise their democratic practices together.

One of these institutions—the library—has a long history of this civic work or *community engagement*—a term that refers to the multiple ways in which we learn about, collaborate with, and support community members.[7] Typical community engagement activities include facilitating community conversations, assessing community aspirations and concerns, involving community members in decision-making, partnering to advance shared goals, promoting civic literacy, convening forums for dialogue and deliberation, and engaging with diverse historic and cultural experiences of constituents. Whereas outreach focuses on extending an organization's reach, engagement begins with building relationships with the community. This chapter will review the history of these concepts and the ways in which libraries have embraced them and provides context for subsequent chapters that describe how such community engagement activities are shaping the future of libraries.

THE REVIVAL OF AMERICAN COMMUNITY: THE CASE FOR A STRONG DEMOCRACY

Robert Putnam's call for the revival of American community popularized a movement that had begun in the late twentieth century. Among the early voices was that of political scientist Benjamin Barber, who prescribed "strong democracy" as a remedy to incivility and apathy, where "active citizens govern themselves in the only form that is genuinely and completely democratic."[8] Barber claimed that "citizens are neighbors bound together neither by blood nor by contract but by their common concerns and common participation in the search for common solutions to common conflicts."[9]

Barber's pioneering work on the revitalization of citizen participation in community affairs was followed by other political scientists who applied practical techniques to this active citizenship model, engaging lay citizens in deliberation about issues of common concern, and developed theories of active citizenship as well, using new models for reinvigorating communities through the creation of free spaces or commons where citizens participate in shaping the public life in their communities.[10] A tidal wave of other civil society theorists has contributed to this scholarship over the past three decades—scholars who are strong proponents of citizen participation in public life, along with a cadre of community builders who have created tools and frameworks for democratic practices that citizens can apply toward renewing their communities.[11]

Democracy and Citizenship

Democracy as we know it originated in ancient Greece twenty-five hundred years ago. The term is derived from the Greek words *demos*, or the people/citizenry, and *-cracy* (from *kratos*), or the power to rule. In Greece and Rome, governance incorporated popular participation by land-owning male citizens, empowering them to shape their future. Democracy's origins as a political system expected citizens to work together to make life better for everyone. In modern democracies, state sovereignty is located in the people, as citizen proprietors, who are responsible for active participation in public affairs.

Our founding fathers did not mention democracy when they declared independence from Britain, but they did start the new Constitution with "We the People," elevating the people's allegiance to each other rather than as subjects to a king. Although restricted initially to land-owning white men, but later expanded to white women and African Americans, the right to participate in federal and local affairs was extended over the centuries to include all who belong to a community. As "citizens" of our democracy, all of us should aspire to work together to solve common problems and produce benefits for everyone.[12]

No single definition of democracy as practiced in America has dominated political discourse. The founders created at the federal level a representative democracy that would delegate decisions to elected legislators; powers not enumerated in the Constitution were left to states and localities. In the nineteenth century, President Abraham Lincoln delivered the Gettysburg Address, speaking of an ideal government that is *of, by, and for the people.* In the following century, American leaders saw democracy through different lenses. President Lyndon Johnson considered democracy to be voting, whereas President Bill Clinton saw it as governing. In contrast, President Franklin Roosevelt embraced participation as central to our democratic processes.

In the twenty-first century, attempts to reclaim a participatory democracy have focused on strategies to bridge some of the divide separating the public from our representative government as a collaborative venture of institutions working *with* citizens, not just for them. In a participatory democracy, authority does not descend from the top down from competing leadership but rises from the bottom up from an undivided base. This grassroots form of democracy begins at a smaller scale locally and offers citizens opportunities to become full-fledged players by examining problems and finding solutions together. In communities, citizens do the "public work" of discussing concerns openly, finding common ground, and making decisions through small, informal groups like clubs, organizations, and other associations. For success, community members must develop social capital—the trusted bonds and bridges that connect those who are both like and unlike them. They also need civic spaces where they feel safe to make mutually beneficial choices, recognize possibilities, and cocreate solutions. Catalytic, boundary-spanning institutions can assist them by bringing them together to learn, build collective knowledge, develop partnerships, and share leadership.

Toward an Informed and Engaged Citizenry

America's founding fathers proclaimed loudly and often the necessity of an informed citizenry in order to exercise their civic responsibilities wisely. This creed of the informed citizenry became a central theme in American life, a conviction that has helped articulate the relationship between citizens and self-governance since the early days of the republic. Also key to the emerging American democracy were the associations and activities that create the glue which strengthens civil society and that ensure a structure and climate for active citizen participation in our democratic system, notably described in the early nineteenth century by French diplomat and political theorist Alexis de Tocqueville.[13] Later in that century, the populace founded libraries, colleges, schools, newspapers, and the post office to inform a growing citizenry. For generations, belief in the role of an informed citizenry has served as a guide-post for these institutions, validating their essential role in promoting political, economic, and social prosperity and in building the capacity for current and future citizens to participate effectively in the processes of democracy.

The Jeffersonian conviction of an informed citizenry, embraced throughout U.S. history, has evolved over time as more and more information has become readily available to all. An informed public constitutes the very foundation of a democracy; after all, democracies are about discourse—discourse among the people. If a free society is to survive, it must ensure the preservation of its records and provide free and open access to this information to all its citizens. Yet historian Richard Brown contends that the broadening of rights to participate in American civic life has changed the definition and meaning of an informed citizenry, resulting in the gradual dissociation of knowledge and citizenship today.[14] Instead, the contemporary notion of an informed citizenry implies simply an initial stage of participatory democracy—a one-way relationship in which government compiles and delivers information to citizens.[15] Sociologist Michael Schudson considers this form of engagement "monitorial" citizenship, whereby citizens only pay attention when things go wrong, and political scientist Benjamin Barber refers to it as "thin democracy," dominated by representative institutions with relatively passive citizens.[16]

A more interactive stage of participation—the consultation stage—constitutes an interactive, two-way relationship between informed citizens and their government, whereby voices are heard through public opinion surveys and commentary related to proposed legislation and regulations. Citizens have an opportunity to express their preferences—a stage that Barber refers to as "plebiscitary democracy."[17]

A third, more active stage of participation occurs when citizens engage directly in the decision- and policy-making process, proposing options and shaping outcomes—a stage that Barber calls "strong democracy," whereby citizens "regard discourse, debate, and deliberation as essential conditions for reaching common ground and arbitrating differences among people in a large, multicultural society."[18] As a remedy to incivility and apathy, this stage, according to Barber, enables active citizens to "govern themselves in 'the only form that is genuinely and completely democratic.'"[19]

Barber's strong democratic practice ideals are reflected in the work of several information theorists who recognize that self-governance requires an engaged as well as informed citizenry. To this end, communications researcher Leah Lievrouw describes an information environment that must shift from "informing" to "involving," contending that an involved—not just informed—citizenry is more likely to participate in democratic political processes. "How can it be that American citizens by and large feel alienated from the very political system they profess to believe in, at the same time that they have an ostensibly unprecedented array of media and information sources at their disposal?" she asks.[20] This approach is reflected by the Knight Commission on the Information Needs of Communities in a Democracy, which stated, "The time has come for new thinking and aggressive action to ensure the information opportunities of America's people, the information health of its communities, and the information vitality of our democracy."[21] Among the commission's recommendations are strengthening the *capacity* of individuals to engage with information and promoting individual *engagement* with information and the public life of the community.

In short, the challenge for democratic participation today is no longer the lack of information but an absence of engagement. Active citizens must not only become well informed about their government and the issues of the day but also "participate fully in our system of self-government, to stand up and be heard. Paramount in this vision are the critical democratic values of openness, inclusion, participation, empowerment, and the common pursuit of truth and the public interest."[22] We need an informed *and* engaged populace if our democracy is to thrive in the twenty-first century.

Participatory Democracy

"Democracy begins at home, and its home is the neighborly community," American philosopher and education reformer John Dewey wrote in 1917.[23] To Dewey, face-to-face interactions in which people work together cooperatively to solve common problems build the foundation of participatory democracy— to work *with* the community, not *on* it or *in* it. Citizens working together in communities find ways to act to solve problems. When these problems are "tame," experts can solve them with measurable desired outcomes, as when doctors set a broken arm. But many of the problems we face are considered "wicked"—shared problems such as poverty, crime, and homelessness that defy simple solutions.

The Charles F. Kettering Foundation has identified six core democratic practices that reveal the "ways citizens can work together—even when they disagree—to solve shared problems":[24]

1. Identifying or naming the issues facing citizens in terms of what is meaningful and valuable to them.
2. Framing issues so that a range of actions are considered and the trade-offs evident.
3. Making decisions deliberatively and weighing the trade-offs among choices to move toward sound public judgment.
4. Identifying and committing civic resources that are available.
5. Organizing civic actions to address a public problem in a complementary and coordinated fashion.
6. Encouraging constant collective learning to maintain momentum.

Another organization that has described democratic practices, the International Association for Public Participation (IAP2), uses a "spectrum" to differentiate the resources citizens need to participate in ordinary public discourse (figure 1.1). The IAP2 spectrum ranges from informing at a lower level of engagement to involving, collaborating with, and empowering future citizens on the issues of the day at higher levels of engagement.[25]

FIGURE 1.1 | **IAP2 SPECTRUM OF PUBLIC PARTICIPATION**

IAP2 Spectrum of Public Participation

iap² international association for public participation

IAP2's Spectrum of Public Participation was designed to assist with the selection of the level of participation that defines the public's role in any public participation process. The Spectrum is used internationally, and it is found in public participation plans around the world.

INCREASING IMPACT ON THE DECISION ⟶

	INFORM	CONSULT	INVOLVE	COLLABORATE	EMPOWER
PUBLIC PARTICIPATION GOAL	To provide the public with balanced and objective information to assist them in understanding the problem, alternatives, opportunities and/or solutions.	To obtain public feedback on analysis, alternatives and/or decisions.	To work directly with the public throughout the process to ensure that public concerns and aspirations are consistently understood and considered.	To partner with the public in each aspect of the decision including the development of alternatives and the identification of the preferred solution.	To place final decision making in the hands of the public.
PROMISE TO THE PUBLIC	We will keep you informed.	We will keep you informed, listen to and acknowledge concerns and aspirations, and provide feedback on how public input influenced the decision.	We will work with you to ensure that your concerns and aspirations are directly reflected in the alternatives developed and provide feedback on how public input influenced the decision.	We will look to you for advice and innovation in formulating solutions and incorporate your advice and recommendations into the decisions to the maximum extent possible.	We will implement what you decide.

© IAP2 International Federation 2018. All rights reserved. 20181112_v1

Likewise, the National Coalition for Dialogue and Deliberation (NCDD) offers a *Streams of Engagement* framework with four different approaches to citizen participation, breaking down participatory processes best suited for specific dialogic circumstances (figure 1.2):

- **Exploration:** community conversations about aspirations and struggles;
- **Conflict Transformation:** poor relations or specific conflict tackled;
- **Decision Making:** decision or policy impacted and public knowledge improved; or

FIGURE 1.2 | **NCDD ENGAGEMENT STREAMS**

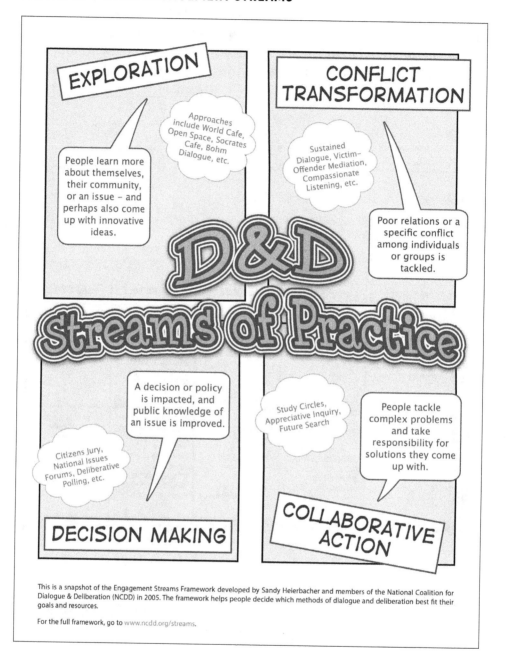

This is a snapshot of the Engagement Streams Framework developed by Sandy Heierbacher and members of the National Coalition for Dialogue & Deliberation (NCDD) in 2005. The framework helps people decide which methods of dialogue and deliberation best fit their goals and resources.

For the full framework, go to www.ncdd.org/streams.

- **Collaborative Action:** complex problems tackled with responsibility for action taken[26]

NCDD also offers a useful typology for considering goals of participatory dialogue, each level moving toward improving civic and community capacity to address issues and take collective action:

1. **First-order goals:** issue learning, improved democratic attitudes and skills
2. **Second-order goals:** individual and community action, improved institutional decision-making, and managed conflicts
3. **Third-order goals:** improved community problem solving, and increased civic capacity[27]

LIBRARIES AND THE CIVIC RENEWAL MOVEMENT

Librarians have long recognized the importance of engaging communities in democratic discourse. Since their founding, libraries have regularly served as "important public spaces for the kinds of meetings and informal gatherings that knit communities together."[28] In the late nineteenth century, public libraries continued "the educational process where the schools left off and by conducting a people's university, a wholesome capable citizenry would be fully schooled in the conduct of a democratic life."[29]

By the 1920s, the idea of libraries as informal education centers that advanced democratic ideals took hold.[30] After World War II, a nationwide discussion program was launched to rejuvenate the democratic spirit in the country, a program that provided ideal opportunities for libraries to assume community leadership roles by spreading "reliable information on all sides of this vital issue and for the encouragement of free discussion and action."[31] In 1952 the American Heritage Project fostered discussions in libraries that considered traditional American values and "demonstrated its belief that loyalty to democracy and commitment to free speech were not only compatible but identical."[32] In that same year, the American Library Association (ALA) joined a national effort to increase voter turnout by distributing election information and organizing activities that positioned public libraries to offer "an experience of democracy as well as a consideration of it."[33]

Not until the late 1980s did libraries around the country resume the convening of local citizens to deliberate about issues of the day. A 1992 *National Issues Forums in Libraries Newsletter* showcased some of these dialogue initiatives

LIBRARIES STRENGTHENING DEMOCRACY

Libraries are adopting innovative approaches to engaging their communities and strengthening democracy, reflecting the IAP2 spectrum that ranges from informing at a lower level of engagement to involving, collaborating with, and empowering future citizens on the issues of the day at higher levels of engagement.

Expanding on their more traditional roles, libraries inform citizens and help them sign up for government services like the Affordable Care Act through model e-Government services, such as those offered at Florida's Pasco County library system. Other libraries, such as Rutgers University Libraries–Camden and the University of Texas at El Paso Library, produce civic engagement LibGuides as starting points for students enrolled in service-learning classes. A University of Kansas community engagement librarian has recorded a Campus Compact webinar showcasing creative ways to increase access to engaged campus scholarship and to build bridges across campus. And at American University, librarians partnered with their student government, development, and alumni relations office and the DC League of Women Voters to develop a toolkit to help more than one thousand students apply for absentee ballots.

Farther along the IAP2 spectrum, librarians are helping students become civic actors by incorporating civic literacy skills into their instructional strategies, such as those at William Paterson University in New Jersey who partner with the campus activities office and student leadership to sponsor an academic learning component for service-learning. At the Urban School in San Francisco, librarian Sarah Jane Levin collaborates with teachers to help students develop critical civic "skills that help our citizen students recognize how to enhance service work and become agents of change in a democratic society."[1]

To facilitate engagement, many libraries have refurbished or built exciting new spaces for their libraries—spaces that also serve as public gathering spots that anchor neighborhoods, downtowns, schools, and campuses. A good example is the public library in Salt Lake City, which built a dramatic new facility designed by Moshe Safdie "to create common ground"—an award-winning facility considered the community gathering place where "citizens practice democracy."[2] Community rooms in many public and academic libraries now serve as the locus for facilitated community conversations that strengthen those libraries' civic missions.

NOTES

1. Sarah Jane Levin, "Student as Citizen: Teaching Critical Civic Literacy Skills in the Library," *Knowledge Quest* 44, no. 5 (May/June, 1966): 29–31.
2. John Berry, "Where Democracy Happens," *Library Journal* 131, no. 11 (June 15, 2006): 32.

that were hosted from New York to California and even featured radio-library forums, which were held in Ohio and Minnesota. Later that decade, echoing broader calls for civic renewal, a cadre of library leaders began advocating a broader new "civic librarianship," in which libraries strengthen democracy by building and renewing communities and engaging citizens in public work.[34]

Moving Libraries from Informing to Engaging Citizens

Today's public, academic, and school libraries are moving from collection-focused to engagement-centered models of service to increase their impact and significance. Leaders across the profession now talk about the need to engage their communities by building partnerships that deliver impact and results, realign their civic missions, and embed their services in their communities. ALA and its Public Library Association, the Urban Libraries Council, the Institute for Museum and Library Services, the International City/County Management Association, and the Aspen Institute have all launched collaborative initiatives to advance community engagement through libraries.

Most notably, ALA's Libraries Transforming Communities initiative, in collaboration with such organizations as the Harwood Institute for Public Innovation and the National Coalition for Dialogue and Deliberation, has trained several thousand librarians in these approaches. "My interest in libraries is that they're essential to the civic life of communities, and . . . libraries still have a great reservoir of trust in communities that a lot of community and public institutions no longer have," Richard Harwood, founder of the Harwood Institute, said shortly after the launch of Libraries Transforming Communities in 2015. "I think they're essential right now to helping us rebuild our sense of connection to one another, and the ability of communities to come together and solve problems together."[35]

Transforming Libraries into Agents of Engagement

Democracy needs libraries to provide opportunities and safe spaces for citizens to engage. Unquestionably, librarians are ready and eager to adopt new practices to align their work with the aspirations and concerns of their communities. Yet, even though libraries are among the most trusted of public institutions, they need to "look carefully at opportunities to strengthen their role in addressing serious problems in their own communities."[36]

The realm of listening to communities and convening public conversations necessitates the adoption of new competencies as well as a shift from a mission that informs citizens to one that also *engages* them.[37] As the nation's great experiment in democracy comes under increasing threat, libraries that transform into agents of a *strong* democracy will bring communities together and empower citizens to participate actively in civic life.

NOTES

1. Robert Putnam, *Bowling Alone: The Collapse and Revival of American Community* (New York: Simon and Schuster, 2000), 27.

2. National Issues Forums Institute, *Democracy's Challenge: Reclaiming the Public Role* (Dayton, OH: National Issues Forums Institute, 2006); and *A House Divided: What Would We Have to Give Up to Get the Political System We Want?* (Dayton, OH: National Issues Forums Institute, 2019), https://www.nifi.org/sites/default/files/product-downloads/A%20House%20Divided%20Digital%20Version.pdf.

3. Pew Research Center, *Public Highly Critical of State of Political Discourse in the U.S.; Reactions to Trump's Rhetoric: Concern, Confusion, Embarrassment* (Washington, DC: Pew Research Center, June 19, 2019), https://www.people-press.org/2019/06/19/public-highly-critical-of-state-of-political-discourse-in-the-u-s/?utm_source=Pew+Research+Center&utm_campaign=8c881f687d-EMAIL_CAMPAIGN_2019_06_21_03_07&utm_medium=email&utm_term=0_3e953b9b70-8c881f687d-400761665.

4. Pew Research Center, *Government Gets Lower Ratings for Handling Health Care, Environment, Disaster Response* (Washington, DC: Pew Research Center, December, 14, 2017), http://assets.pewresearch.org/wp-content/uploads/sites/5/2017/12/14104805/12-14-17-Government-release.pdf.

5. Pew Research Center, *The Public, the Political System, and American Democracy* (Washington, DC: Pew Research Center, April 26, 2018), https://www.people-press.org/2018/04/26/1-democracy-and-government-the-u-s-political-system-elected-officials-and-governmental-institutions/.

6. Doble Research Associates, *Public Thinking about Democracy's Challenge: Reclaiming the Public's Role* (Dayton, OH: Kettering Foundation, 2006); and John Doble and Jean Johnson, *A House Divided? Reflections on the Public's Mood* (Dayton, OH: Kettering Foundation, 2017), https://www.kettering.org/catalog/product/house-divided.

7. The Centers for Disease Control and Prevention defines *community engagement* as "the process of working collaboratively with and through groups of people affiliated by geographic proximity, special interest, or similar situations to address issues affecting the wellbeing of those people. . . . It often involves partnerships and coalitions that help mobilize resources and influence systems, change relationships among partners, and serve as catalysts for changing policies, programs, and practices." Centers for Disease Control and Prevention, *Principles of Community Engagement*, 1st ed. (Atlanta,

GA: CDC/ATSDR Committee on Community Engagement, 1997), 9. The Tamarack Institute for Community Engagement uses this definition: "people working collaboratively, through inspired action and learning, to create and realize bold visions for their common future." Tamarack Institute, *Our Growing Understanding of Community Engagement* (Waterloo, Ontario: Tamarack Institute, n.d.), https://cdn2.hubspot.net/hubfs/316071/Resources/Article/Our_Growing_Understanding_of_Community _Engagement.pdf.

8. Benjamin Barber, *Strong Democracy: Participatory Politics for a New Age* (Berkeley, CA: University of California Press, 1984), 148.

9. Barber, *Strong Democracy*, 219.

10. Notable among these scholars are David Mathews, *Engaging Citizens: Meeting the Challenges of Community Life* (Dayton, OH: Kettering Foundation, 2006), http://kettering .org/wp-content/uploads/EngagingCitizens.pdf; and Harry Boyte, *Everyday Politics: The Power of Public Work* (Philadelphia: University of Pennsylvania, 2004).

11. Illustrative of this movement to revitalize democracy are Daniel Yankelovich, *Coming to Public Judgment: Making Democracy Work in a Complex World* (Syracuse, NY: Syracuse University Press, 1991); Daniel Yankelovich and Will Friedman, eds., *Toward Wiser Public Judgment* (Nashville, TN: Vanderbilt University Press, 2010); and Archon Fong, *Empowered Participation: Reinventing Urban Democracy* (Princeton, NJ: Princeton University Press, 2004). Pioneers in shaping new approaches to engaging communities were John Kretzmann and John McKnight, *Building Communities from the Inside Out: A Path Toward Finding and Mobilizing Community Assets* (London, UK: ACTA Publications, 1997).

12. For purposes of this discussion, "'citizen,' as the term is employed here, is used in its historic sense—all the people who live in a city, village, or community. They are the demos or collective citizenry in 'democracy.' The term is not used in the narrow, legalistic sense." David Mathews, *With the People: Making Democracy Work as It Should* (Dayton, OH: Cousins Research Group, Kettering Foundation, 2019), 4, https://www .kettering.org/sites/default/files/product-downloads/with_the_people_crg.pdf.

13. Alexis de Tocqueville, *Democracy in America* (New York: Vintage Books, 1990).

14. Richard Brown, *The Strength of a People: The Idea of an Informed Citizenry in America, 1650–1870* (Chapel Hill: University of North Carolina Press, 1996), 196–207.

15. Organisation for Economic Co-operation and Development (OECD), *Citizens as Partners: Information, Consultation and Public Participation in Policy-Making* (Paris, France: OECD, 2001), https://www.oecd-ilibrary.org/governance/citizens-as-partners _9789264195561-en.

16. Michael Schudson, *The Good Citizen: A History of American Civic Life* (New York: The Free Press, 1998); Michael Schudson, "Click Here for Democracy: A History and Critique of an Information-Based Model of Citizenship," in *Democracy and New Media*, ed. Henry Jenkins and David Thorburn (Cambridge, MA: MIT Press, 2003), 49–59; and Benjamin Barber, *Strong Democracy*.

17. Benjamin Barber, "Which Technology and Which Democracy?," in *Democracy and New Media*, ed. Henry Jenkins and David Thorburn (Cambridge, MA: MIT Press, 2003), 33–47.

18. Barber, *Strong Democracy*; Barber, "Which Technology and Which Democracy?," 37.

19. Barber, *Strong Democracy*, 148.

20. Leah Lievrouw, "Information Resources and Democracy: Understanding the Paradox," *Journal of the American Society for Information Science* 45, no. 6 (1994): 350.

21. Knight Commission on the Information Needs of Communities in a Democracy, *Informing Communities: Sustaining Democracy in the Digital Age* (Washington, DC: The Aspen Institute, 2009), 1, https://assets.aspeninstitute.org/content/uploads/files/content/docs/pubs/Informing_Communities_Sustaining_Democracy_in_the_Digital_Age.pdf.

22. Knight Commission, *Informing Communities*, 2.

23. John Dewey, *The Public and Its Problems* (New York: H. Holt, 1927).

24. David Mathews, *The Ecology of Democracy: Finding Ways to Have a Stronger Hand in Shaping Our Future* (Dayton, OH: Kettering Foundation, 2014), 119–25.

25. International Association for Public Participation (IAP2), "IAP2 Spectrum of Public Participation," 2018, https://cdn.ymaws.com/www.iap2.org/resource/resmgr/pillars/Spectrum_8.5x11_Print.pdf.

26. National Coalition for Dialogue and Deliberation, *Streams for Engagement*, rev. ed. (Boiling Springs, PA: NCDD, 2013).

27. Sandy Heierbacher, "New Framework for Understanding the Goals of Public Engagement," *NCDD Blog*, July 28, 2009, http://ncdd.org/1571.

28. Wayne A. Wiegand, *Main Street Public Library: Community Places and Reading Spaces in the Rural Heartland, 1876–1956* (Iowa City: University of Iowa Press, 2011), 180.

29. Sidney Ditzion, *Arsenals of a Democratic Culture: A Social History of the American Public Library Movement in New England and the Middle States from 1850 to 1900* (Chicago: American Library Association, 1947), 74.

30. Willian S. Learned, *The American Public Library and the Diffusion of Knowledge* (New York: Harcourt, Brace and Company, 1924).

31. Jean Preer, "Promoting Citizenship: How Librarians Helped Get Out the Vote in the 1952 Election," *Libraries and the Cultural Record* 43, no. 1 (Spring 2008): 3. Preer quotes Ruth Rutzen, chair of ALA's Adult Education Board.

32. Jean Preer, "The American Heritage Project: Librarians and the Democratic Tradition in the Early Cold War," *Libraries and Culture* 28, no. 2 (Spring 1993): 166.

33. Jean Preer, "Exploring the American Idea at the New York Public Library," *American Studies* 42, no. 3 (Fall 2001): 151.

34. Among the books published at that time: Kathleen de la Peña McCook, *A Place at the Table: Participating in Community Building* (Chicago: American Library Association, 2000); Ronald McCabe, *Civic Librarianship: Renewing the Social Mission of the Public Library* (Lanham, MD: Scarecrow Press, 2001); and Nancy Kranich, *Libraries and Democracy: Cornerstones of Liberty* (Chicago: American Library Association, 2001).

35. Lisa Peet, "Rich Harwood on Libraries as Change Agents, Turning Outward, and the Need for Qualitative Data," *Library Journal* (January 9, 2015), https://theharwood institute.org/news/2015/01/rich-harwood-in-the-library-journal-about-libraries-as -change-agents.

36. Public Agenda, *Long Overdue: A Fresh Look at Public and Leadership Attitudes about Libraries in the 21st Century* (New York: Public Agenda, 2006), 13, https://www.public agenda.org/files/Long_Overdue.pdf.

37. ALA's Libraries Transforming Communities initiative offers many webinars and tools to develop skills to convene, facilitate, and engage communities, available at www.ala.org/LTC. See also Center for Engaged Democracy Core Competencies Committee, *Core Competencies in Civic Engagement: A Working Paper in the Center for Engaged Democracy's Policy Papers Series* (North Andover, MA: Merrimack College Center for Engaged Democracy, 2012), https://www.merrimack.edu/live/files/160-core -competencies-in-civic-engagement; and Beverly Sheppard, K. Flinner, R. J. Norlander, and Mary Davis Fournier, *National Impact of Library Public Programs Assessment: Phase 1, A White Paper on the Dimensions of Library Programs and the Skills and Training for Library Program Professionals*, NewKnowledge Publication #IML.074.207.07 (Chicago: American Library Association and New Knowledge Organization, 2019), https://nilppa.org/wp-content/uploads/2019/06/NILPPA_Phase-1-white-paper.pdf.

EMPOWERING COMMUNITIES
From Public Trust to Impact

ERICA FREUDENBERGER *and* SUSAN HILDRETH

ibraries are part of socio-ecosystems, and they can only be as strong as the whole. How can libraries leverage their trusted role in the community? As anchor institutions, libraries can play a critical role in convening and facilitating conversations about what matters to people. Libraries can create pathways to empower people to take agency in their lives and communities and make the change they want to see in the world. By playing a role as a catalyst, fostering democracy, collaborating with other stakeholders for collective impact, making connections between organizations, or convening conversations, libraries can claim a place at the table and be a part of the decision-making impacting their communities.

INVOLVING, NOT SERVING

Early navigators traversing the Hudson River were dazzled by a bend in the river where maple trees displayed fiery red leaves and dubbed the area "Red Hook." Centuries later, people are still drawn to the area because of its natural beauty, as well as its rich history, old buildings, quaint neighborhoods, and active community. Kids walk to school on the same bluestone sidewalks their parents walked decades earlier, people leave their doors unlocked, and community celebrations are common. Bard College brings an influx of international and artistic students, who are quickly charmed by, if not fully integrated into, community life. Second-home owners flock to Red Hook for its natural beauty and proximity to Bard College, which provides robust cultural attractions—including a Frank Gehry building, famous professors (Neil Gaiman!), and theatrical performances.

In autumn 2016 the Red Hook Town Board in New York's Hudson Valley passed a law limiting the number of drive-through and formula businesses that could be established. The language of the bill cited the work done by the Red Hook Public Library during conversations with residents identifying what they valued and the community's vision of itself and its future. Residents, the library had learned, valued small-town life and were reluctant to bring in big-box stores that would crush the vibrant small, local businesses that had begun to take root.

The library had in 2014 been accepted as part of the American Library Association's Libraries Transforming Communities cohort, a group of ten public libraries from communities of various sizes and demographics that spent eighteen months learning community engagement strategies and putting them to work on topics of local concern. As part of our work, library staff went door-to-door to talk to residents about the future of the village and discuss strategies for creating a resilient community. Despite what experts and some property owners thought best—attracting large-scale retailers as a plan to boost the economy—residents disagreed. Instead, they took action to ensure that Red Hook would continue to thrive while retaining the essential character and charm they loved.

What the library had done was a simple idea: it brought people together to talk about what mattered to them, then compiled the data and shared it widely, sparking a more extensive discussion about the future of Red Hook. As people met to talk, they realized there was more that united than divided them and that they had a set of shared values. By convening conversations that brought disparate voices to the table and identifying what people wanted to happen in the coming decades, the library was recognized as a valuable stakeholder committed to working *with* the community, in contrast to the more traditional role of the library as working *for* the community.

This distinction gets to the power dynamic between organizations and people. Too often, we library workers see ourselves as doing things *for* our communities, as if residents were passive players who benefit from our expertise and actions. Doing things *for* others brings with it paternalistic overtones, as if we know better and have better insight into what people want and need than they do. When we make a conscious decision to provide community members with the information and tools they need to make the changes they desire, they become active agents in democracy.

Community engagement involves opening up library processes not only to serve constituents but to involve them in the process of identifying and meeting community needs. This goal requires library workers to relinquish some control of programs and share ownership with the community. As a result, libraries are able to empower their communities to become their partners in making change.

LIBRARY AS CATALYST

As Randolph, Vermont, saw the closure of several cornerstone businesses in late 2017 and early 2018, Amy Grasmick, the director of the Kimball Public Library, partnered with the Randolph Community Development Corporation to convene a Downtown Discussion. The Kimball Public Library serves the towns of Randolph, a community of 4,700, and Braintree, which has 1,105 residents. As the largest town in Orange County, Vermont, Randolph draws people from surrounding towns to do their shopping, receive social services, bank, and visit restaurants. Primarily agricultural, the town is in the process of determining new opportunities for businesses to bolster employment in the region.

The in-person gathering was a response to a discussion that had already been gaining momentum online. When the organizers behind Front Porch Forum, an electronic discussion platform that strives to help neighbors connect and build community, hosted a moderated online discussion about challenges facing Randolph, more than one hundred people took part. At the time, the overarching narrative was that the town was in crisis, and, as Grasmick says, "a feeling that it was the end of the world." One participant painted a bleak picture:

> Downtown Randolph is dying a slow death, just like most small and medium downtowns across the country. To say that Exit 4 [at I-89, about four miles away from downtown Randolph] development would have killed downtown denies the reality that it is no longer 1950 and that the retail landscape has morphed away from brick and mortar to online. As we will see, preserving the Exit 4 property will not result in any benefit to downtown.[1]

But others, including Grasmick, disagreed and chose to focus on possibilities, not problems. One optimistic resident wrote,

> I love these posts about what people would like to see downtown. Thank you to John [Pimental, who participated in leading the Downtown Discussion with the library and Randolph Area Community Development Corporation] and others for leading this discussion. FPF [Front Porch Forum] is a wonderful place for this and hopefully just the beginning.

I'm new in town and the open [retail] spaces are in some ways exciting because there seems to be a lot of opportunity, but also scary because there's too many open spaces and too many mentions of things people miss in downtown. How can we keep this conversation going, focus on the opportunities, and make something happen?[2]

Grasmick focused the conversation on identifying community assets, asking people what they wanted to see and, most important, what they could do to help bring about the changes they envisioned. At the in-person conversation in February 2018, the library hosted a brainstorming session about the community's vision of its ideal downtown. "Bring your ideas, your optimism, and your willingness to listen," the event description on the library's website read. "This is an opportunity to discuss a bright future rather than dwell on the past, so please leave any negativity or complaints at home."

"The best part of the whole conversation was that people were encouraging each other to start businesses, and they could get immediate feedback from their friends and neighbors," said Grasmick. The Downtown Discussion proved to be a turning point for the community, revitalizing and energizing people to take a chance on a new business; to date, a bike shop, a restaurant, and a café have opened. For Grasmick, taking on the challenge was initially daunting, but she saw it as "a new experience to step so far outside of what I perceived of my role as the library director."[3]

Grasmick was surprised to find that she enjoyed encouraging people to share their ideas and helping them find ways to implement those ideas. Asking people what they could do to contribute to the process was a crucial part of that engagement. Her experience has prompted her to try new ways of engaging her community. Most recently, she's placed several large sticky notes at a barbershop, a bowling alley, and other places people congregate in town. On each, she has one question: "If you had $200,000 to spend on the Kimball Library, what would you do?"

Grasmick points to Front Porch Forum, the electronic discussion list, as an essential tool. As a place for people to gather and share ideas, it provides her with an ongoing bird's-eye view of what matters to people in her town. She can identify the people who are interested in taking action on matters that concern them and are able to do so. People with similar interests can organize, and the library can step in with information and resources as needed.

As a result of a mobilized and engaged community, the Town of Randolph was selected as a "Climate Economy Model Community" by the Vermont Council on Rural Development, which provided a full year of mentoring for community members to seize the reins of the region's economic and environmental future. The process—dubbed the Randolph Region Re-Energized, or R3—was built on action items identified by the Downtown Discussion. An unexpected benefit of the process was a partnership between the Friends of the Kimball Library and the new café in town. People wanted a bookstore in town, and, as a result of this partnership, the library was able to sell its used books at the café. Grasmick reports that both town government officials and private citizens were grateful to have an opportunity to discuss the future positively, to take action that moved their community forward in a positive way.

Sound simple? Well, it is, and it isn't. Convening conversations takes time, thought, and planning; a conversation is only as good as the facilitator and participants, and for it to be meaningful, everyone must have a clear idea of what the conversation is trying to accomplish. Grasmick's Downtown Discussion was a success because she did critical planning before it began. She identified potential partners who would be able to take action, established a goal, decided on the format of the discussion, created ground rules, and spent time marketing the process. When the conversation ended, she gathered the data, analyzed it, and prepared it for public distribution and comment.

Although Grasmick had done the heavy lifting of setting the stage, implementing the discussion, and organizing the data collected, she did not make any decisions about how to proceed without first reporting back to the community to ensure that the plans being developed were resonating with them. Her work helped steer the town away from an abyss of fear about the future to a place of empowerment where community members could identify the steps they needed to take to ensure that they could boldly move forward in a positive, purposeful way.

HOW DO YOU LEARN ABOUT YOUR COMMUNITY?

For those who aren't sure where to begin, fear not. Ample resources are available to help you get started using the community engagement model.

- An excellent place to begin is by learning all you can about your community, directly from your community. Consider digital resources. In Randolph, Vermont, Front Porch Forum (https://frontporchforum.com/) was a place where Grasmick could take the pulse of her community.
- Social media offer great starting places. Many communities have lively discussions on informal Facebook pages. In Red Hook, the Red Hook Moms Facebook forum had regular discussions about a wide range of community issues.
- And finally, attending local meetings, whether formal or informal, and asking questions about what matters to people yields fruitful results.

TAKING ACTION

When Lisa Sammet, the director of the Jeudevine Memorial Library in Hardwick, Vermont, began hosting programs on climate change, organic gardening, composting, genetically modified organisms, and honeybees, she didn't expect the result to be legislation.[4] But that's what happened. The town of three thousand, founded in the eighteenth century, was eager to learn how to live in a way that would ensure that the community and land would be healthy for generations.

As people began to implement what they had learned at the library's programs by applying organic gardening methods, their concerns about pesticides containing neonicotinoids, which kill honeybees and other pollinators, grew. Sammet invited the community's state representative to host meetings at the library, where the community could discuss the impact of neonicotinoids on bees. In response to the community's concerns, the state representative introduced legislation to the House of Representatives, and people followed up with calls to make their case to other representatives. In June 2019 the bill passed both chambers and was signed by Governor Phil Scott, significantly restricting the use of neonicotinoids.

Sammet—like Grasmick some fifty miles south—identified community concerns and developed library programs to stimulate discussion and spur action. Her series of programs on the environment identifying the relationship between local and global environmental concerns did just that. Locals embraced organic gardening and composting, choosing to eliminate pesticides in their immediate environs. The next step was legislation banning pesticides containing neonicotinoids. The library convened an ongoing dialogue between its state representative and the community. Residents supported the legislation by continuing to advocate, building a chorus of empowered citizens who were committed to taking action.

What Sammet achieved doesn't happen by accident. It requires deliberate, strategic choices about how to frame conversations, supply information, and invite stakeholders to the table. It's organizing people to make educated decisions about their lives and take action that impacts their lives—a concept essential to our ideal of democracy.

IDENTIFYING AND MEETING COMMUNITY NEEDS

Sacramento, California, the state capital, is one of the fastest-growing communities on the West Coast with more than four hundred thousand residents. Almost two decades ago, *Time* magazine named it one of the most diverse cities in the country.[5] As people flock to the area, drawn by the exceptional higher education and opportunities to work in the health-care, state government, and tourism industries, new challenges arise.

To meet the needs of this expanding, diverse population, the Sacramento Public Library adopted an approach to community engagement promoted by the Harwood Institute for Public Innovation. One of the library's first initiatives, spurred by library staff who have children or family members with special needs, was to engage the special needs community—kids and families dealing with autism, and adults with special needs. Traditionally, the library had two challenges when serving this population:

1. The library was not providing adequate services for this community.
2. Some staff were not comfortable working with customers with special needs.

The library held six community conversations and several one-on-one interviews with adults and youth in the Sacramento area. Librarians engaged families with special needs and their allies, making a point to include people who weren't library users. As organizers aggregated what they had heard in the conversations, key themes emerged. Special needs adults and families

- Wanted to be accepted and included in their community
- Needed a central, trusted hub of information and resources
- Needed more opportunities to become involved in community activities and programs

To address these clear community priorities, the library significantly altered its products and services. Seven branches were identified as "hub libraries" to serve as models of inclusion, complete with staff accessibility experts. At these locations the library launched accessible sensory storytimes, services focused on adults with disabilities, inclusive family movies, and volunteer programs. To continue the library's effort, staff accessibility experts from hub libraries train employees from other branches to provide inclusive programming and guidance and to develop partnerships with community organizations serving the special needs community.

To further reinforce this commitment, the library offered staff seven training sessions over five months that focused on disability awareness and available services. The effort was highly successful, with 87 percent of library staff reporting that they felt more confident providing excellent customer service to people with disabilities.

LIBRARY AS PLATFORM

Seattle, Washington, a city of more than seven hundred thousand in the Pacific Northwest, had a history of "excessive force and racially biased policing within the Seattle Police Department. . . . Growing distrust of the local criminal justice system was felt by many Seattle communities, leading to community-led protests in 2016 over the decision to build a new Juvenile Detention facility in Seattle."[6] In response to the dissent, the Seattle Public Library began engaging with prison abolitionists, community activists who want to build a society that does not need prisons. The library also works with legal advocates and other community partners who are committed to bringing social justice issues to the forefront in their community. The library regularly convenes talks by civil rights leaders as well as panel discussions and community listening sessions that bring together diverse voices and viewpoints. It also provides more traditional library services by offering resources and programs exploring social justice issues, including civil rights, intellectual freedom, and the criminal justice system.

These library efforts relied on a community-led process that placed individuals who were directly affected by criminal justice at the center of program development with library staff playing a supporting role. By doing so, the library not only removes the abstraction of the impact of the criminal justice system by linking faces, names, and families to the issue. In convening community-wide conversations, the library acts as a platform to amplify values that are important to its community and facilitates opportunities for residents to come together and find equitable, compassionate solutions.

Valerie Wonder, in "Civic Engagement through Community-Led Programming," says, "As we work in this way, the library begins the slow institutional work of moving beyond the practice of information sharing and awareness-raising that serves a relatively privileged audience toward a practice of empowerment and of accountability to communities most affected by the social justice issue at hand."[7]

By exploring these crucial topics, holding public events, leveraging its resources, and asking court-involved youth and adults, along with their families, to share how mass incarceration has affected them, the library has provided space and a platform for community involvement. The broader community has been asked to join the conversation to discuss challenging topics like the school-to-prison pipeline and bail reform. The library has strengthened Seattle's commitment to imagining a world without prisons and a world in which people and communities are whole, healthy, inclusive, and interconnected. In Seattle, this vision now means its residents have committed to zero youth detention.

RECLAIMING THE NARRATIVE

In 2004 the Vancouver (British Columbia) Public Library partnered with the Halifax (Nova Scotia) Public Libraries, the Toronto (Ontario) Public Library, the Regina (Saskatchewan) Public Library, and Human Resources and Social Development Canada to launch the Working Together Project. The idea was to identify ways libraries could use a community development approach to work with low-income communities. The project sought to establish relationships and work with socially excluded communities to identify and respond to their information needs; identify systemic barriers to library use for socially excluded people; and determine what structural and procedural changes needed to take place to dismantle the identified barriers.[8]

The Working Together Project recognized that libraries have a class problem. Middle- and upper-middle-class patrons receive excellent services and tend to be regular library users. Low-income people are often more reluctant to use the library for many reasons—including but not limited to fines, policies, codes of conduct, and the design and organization of space—all of which magnify the feeling of social exclusion. This quandary isn't unique to Canadian libraries—finding ways to reach and serve nonusers is a perennial topic of conversation in U.S. libraries as well. By proactively naming and addressing the issue and acknowledging when libraries are failing to create equitable spaces, we can commit to making room for multiple voices and experiences. Recognizing the disparity is the first step in building trust. The next, more important step is taking action to remedy the inequality.

COLLECTIVE IMPACT

When communities are confronted with large, systemic challenges, multiple stakeholders may have a role to play. And though the library can serve as the primary catalyst for community engagement, another approach is civic improvement through collective impact. This work is based on the belief that large-scale social change comes from better cross-sector coordination rather than isolated intervention of individual organizations. Based on a commitment of a group of leaders from different sectors to a common agenda for solving a specific social problem, collective impact projects use a centralized infrastructure, dedicated staff, and a structured process to create a "backbone support organization." Libraries can serve as valuable partners in these collaborations, as in the case of the Azusa City Library in Los Angeles County, California.[9]

In 2013 the library created Grassroots ESL, a library-led collaboration dedicated to providing English for Speakers of Other Languages (ESOL) services to the nearly twenty-five thousand residents of Azusa City (total population of forty-six thousand) who did not speak English. As its original partners fell by the wayside, the library realized it wasn't enough to serve as a capacity builder and convener of stakeholders. It received a 2016 Sparks! Ignition grant from the Institute of Museum and Library Services to learn more about the collective impact model. The library created a model for partnership that included a common agenda with a shared vision and measurements for all stakeholders. All the participating organizations agreed to mutually reinforcing activities, which did not have to be uniform across different agencies but did have to work toward the shared vision and agenda. Communication, as with less formal collaborations, was key, as was building trust. And everyone involved—from stakeholders to students—had to benefit from the collaboration, rather than feeling that they were working toward someone else's goal.

The collective impact model was implemented successfully in Azusa City. Grassroots ESL is now a community program, with shared ownership and responsibility. The library credits the success of its program to transparent leadership, a willingness to engage with and make space for the community in the initiative, and the monitoring of practices and processes to ensure that they are inclusive.

Although this approach leads to a common agenda, shared measurement, continuous communication, and mutually reinforcing activities, it may be a heavy lift for communities that are not highly resourced or do not have access to private or grant funding.

Rich Harwood, an advocate for libraries as boundary-spanning institutions, voiced some concerns regarding the collective impact approach to community change: "No matter how many leaders and organizations join an effort or how well-thought-out and rigorous their plan, it is simply not possible to *impose* a strategy on a community. To be successful, they need to work *with* the community. But how do we ensure that the context of the community itself—its *civic culture*—is part of these efforts to ensure success?"[10] Collective impact initiatives must include an authentic community voice to be truly successful.

BE THE CHANGE

Community engagement is a deliberate, democratic process that welcomes all members of the public, acknowledging that their expertise, talent, and knowledge are abundant. Librarians have an essential role to play in curating and organizing the endless potential of our communities. We must be willing to relinquish our power and control and invite people to take ownership of the library by playing an active role in its leadership, planning, and programming and by identifying valued services. And we have to allow time to build trust, deepening relationships with partners and the community so that we are seen not only as reliable collaborators but as colleagues truly invested in the well-being of our communities.

By engaging our communities and centering our work on their aspirations, we acknowledge that libraries are part of a larger socio-ecosystem and can thrive only when the community does. We cannot expect to have vibrant, sustainable libraries in struggling communities; we do not exist in vacuums. So how do we create democratic organizations that include all of our community? We can begin, says Brian Campbell, by collaborating as equals with community members as we plan library services and by investing time in building relationships and coming to an authentic understanding of our community. "It means moving toward a model in which every user is viewed as a complex individual, with history and community, requiring human contact to fully meet their needs. Such a transformation shifts the library back to its human roots."[11]

When Lisa Sammet chose to host programs about climate change and organic gardening, it wasn't a neutral decision. It was a deliberate effort to educate her community about the ecological changes that were happening and helping community members realize that they weren't powerless in the face of adversity. The Seattle Public Library, working with partners to focus on criminal justice, wanted to highlight challenging issues in its community and find out how the library could make a difference. Because the library provided deliberative forums in public space, people were able to assemble and discuss issues face to face. The library created an opportunity for people in its community to take agency and demand action on a critical issue by providing space to hold conversations, to build trust and relationships so that when it was time for action, people were confident about the direction in which they were moving.

We see that this approach works in the example of the Sacramento Public Library, which made a deliberate effort to understand the aspirations of special needs adults and families, or in the decision of the Village Board of Red Hook to limit formula and drive-through businesses in response to what it heard through community conversations. Recognizing and valuing our shared humanity is at the core of democracy, acknowledging our interdependent and mutual relationships that structure our society. By appreciating the input, expertise, and experience of all community members through open discussion, public libraries become essential players at every decision-making table. When we open our doors, leaving behind our offices or the circulation desk to connect with our communities, we have a chance to model what democratic organizations can achieve—and create the change we want to see in the world.

NOTES

1. Amy Grasmick, e-mail message to author, May 16, 2019.
2. Grasmick, e-mail message to author.
3. Grasmick, e-mail message to author.
4. Lisa Sammet, e-mail message to author, July 3, 2019.
5. Ron Stodghill and Amanda Bower, "Welcome to America's Most Diverse City," *Time*, August 25, 2002, http://content.time.com/time/nation/article/0%2C8599%2C340694% 2C00.html?artId=34.
6. Valerie Wonder, "Civic Engagement through Community-Led Programming," *Public Libraries Online* (March 5, 2018), http://publiclibrariesonline.org/2018/03/civic -engagement-through-community-led-programming/.
7. Wonder, "Civic Engagement."
8. Sandra Singh, "Introduction," *Community-Led Libraries Toolkit* (Vancouver, BC: Vancouver Public Library, 2008), 7, https://www.vpl.ca/sites/vpl/public/Community -Led-Libraries-Toolkit.pdf; Kenneth Williment, "It Takes a Community to Build a Library," *Public Libraries Online* (April 26, 2013), http://publiclibrariesonline.org/ 2013/04/it-takes-a-community-to-build-a-library.
9. Azusa City Library, *Moving from Collaboration to Partnership: An Exploration at the Azusa City Library* (Azusa, CA: Institute of Museum and Library Services, 2016), https://www.ci.azusa.ca.us/DocumentCenter/View/37497/Moving-from-Collaboration Azusa---City-Library?bidId=.
10. Rich Harwood, "Putting Community in Collective Impact," *Stanford Social Innovation Review* (April 7, 2014), https://ssir.org/articles/entry/putting_community_in_collective _impact.
11. Brian Campbell, "Preface," *Community-Led Libraries Toolkit* (Vancouver, BC: Vancouver Public Library, 2008), 8, https://www.vpl.ca/sites/vpl/public/Community-Led-Libraries -Toolkit.pdf.

I'M LISTENING
Reimagining the Book Club Model

HADIYA EVANS

The Denver (Colorado) Public Library's R.A.D.A. (Read. Awareness. Dialogue. Action.) series provides a safe space to discuss some of the issues and movements of the day with respect and compassion. The unique reading and discussion series was created when librarians listened to their community members, who were struggling with the police killings of African Americans around the country—an example of community engagement in itself. But the discussions have provided another listening opportunity for library staff because participants voice their concerns about current events through literature.

THE CATALYST

In 2014 James Davis and Evi Klett, librarians at the Denver Public Library, were confronted with the often blurred lines between library neutrality and personal conviction involving the national discourse surrounding the deaths of Michael Brown (August 9, 2014) and Eric Garner (July 17, 2014), and later Freddie Gray (April 19, 2015) and Sandra Bland (July 13, 2015), at the hands of police. Davis and Klett were repeatedly left feeling helpless when faced with the pain and frustration shared by customers who expressed their need for an outlet to discuss and process the social justice issues occurring on the national level but also in Denver's communities.

Davis and Klett felt a gut-wrenching need to do something more than just lend an empathetic ear. Eventually they concluded that they could no longer remain on the sidelines of devastating issues like police brutality. They both felt strongly that as citizens of Denver and librarians they could do more to engage the community with intention in social justice topics and provide a safe and responsible space to have real, meaningful, and sincere conversations.

The R.A.D.A. social issue book group and discussion model was developed to fill a gap in community engagement and program development at the Denver Public Library. This was uncharted territory for the library, one of the first instances that a program was specifically created in direct response to what Davis and Klett heard repeatedly from multiple customers: the need to discuss and understand. The R.A.D.A. social justice book club and discussion group would, despite initial concerns, fearlessly unpack issues affecting communities the library serves.

R.A.D.A.'s mission is to encourage participants to read for social conscious-ness, so that through a facilitated discussion about a specific topic, there is an exchange of ideas and sharing through books and resources that inspire indi-vidual or collective activism. Each component of the name—Read. Awareness. Dialogue. Action.—clearly outlined what we saw, felt, and heard our community wanted, filling a need that empowered people to speak in a responsible space and trusted environment. Our desire is to inspire participants to be the change they wish to see in their community.

PLANNING AND DEVELOPMENT

Over the course of roughly four months, a committee of interested library staff members (including founding members Davis and Klett) met regularly to move the seedling idea from concept to reality. The committee discussed the feasibil-ity and logistics of what the program would look like, who would facilitate the discussions, and how, when, and where the discussions would take place. To ensure that we are being responsive to the communities we serve, discussion topics are determined by the current socioeconomic climate and localized to Denver, and discussions are facilitated by two R.A.D.A. committee members. Titles selected are required to meet the following criteria: fit the topic, published in the last five years, at least three or more copies available in the system, and written in an accessible style.

A critical component of the book group and discussion model is the moti-vation to action. The term *action* is subjective and defined by the individual. We preface each discussion with this statement: "We invite everyone to engage in a form of action in however way makes sense for you."

The level of involvement looks different for each person and can be applied in a variety of ways. For this reason, we supply a list of diverse resources to share with participants at each discussion that are specific to the topic and offer further investigation. Resources include books, articles, organizations, and websites. R.A.D.A. has become a space that is safe, brave, and responsible, using a variety of resources to analyze concepts and explore theories pertaining to social justice issues.

TEST PILOTING R.A.D.A.

It was decided that we would soft-launch R.A.D.A. during October and November 2015 with two pilot programs on the topics of mass incarceration and the negative perceptions of young males of color rooted in fear and racism, then evaluate to decide whether we would continue. We chose to support the pilot programs with the title selections *The New Jim Crow: Mass Incarceration in the Age of Colorblindness* by Michelle Alexander and *The Griots of Oakland: Voices from the African American Oral History Project,* edited by Angela Zusman.

Both programs exceeded our expectations in terms of attendance, the quality of the discussion, and participants' willingness to open up and speak from their lived experiences on topics that were emotionally triggering and uncomfortable. We've adopted the mantra as a committee that we want our participants to "become comfortable with being uncomfortable." We intentionally invite participants to lean into the space of discomfort to begin the process of learning from a place of empathy.

In order to create this environment, we've established a space that normalizes intense conversations by incorporating a discussion model dedicated to ensuring that participants feel safe and encouraged to be brave via discussion guidelines. The following guidelines are used to reinforce the safety of the space and as shared understanding for dialogue:

- Listen actively; seek first to understand.
- Keep an open mind.
- Be respectful and honest in communication.
- Be mindful of others and do not dominate the discussion.
- Speak your truth without blame or judgment.
- Critique ideas, not people.

To date, the R.A.D.A. committee has hosted fifteen discussions in ten Denver communities, ranging from police brutality, poverty, mental health, and immigration to white supremacy and gentrification.

R.A.D.A.'S EVOLUTION

In February 2018 we held a R.A.D.A. book discussion that addressed the topic of the legacy and symbols of white supremacy and racism using the book *White Rage: The Unspoken Truth of Our Racial Divide* by Carol Anderson. The conversation took place in a Denver community that was at the center of a name change debate due to the namesake's membership in the Ku Klux Klan during the 1920s.

What we heard at this discussion were feelings of frustration and the need for tools to empower bystanders and upstanders when confronted with situations of macro- and microaggressive behavior. In response, the library created a workshop to empower residents to stand up for their neighbors in situations where they faced racism.

For the workshop concept, we employed the same strategy that we had used with the early discussions, first testing participant interest with a pilot to establish a baseline. The pilot workshop focused on using attendees' real-life personal examples to create practice scenarios for navigating awkward conversations about race, avoiding microaggressions and missteps, and gaining clarity on how to proceed with respectful and collaborative dialogue. Our hope was to provide attendees with tools to combat or disrupt these types of aggressive situations in a public, familiar, or business/professional setting.

Our next workshop is a specific request from the Denver Public Library's Children's Department to create a four-part series that tackles the topic, "How to Talk with Kids about Race." In these interactive workshops, adults explore their own messages about race and discuss strategies that engage children in meaningful dialogue. The series provides historical and contemporary context, resources, and tools on the topics of confronting personal bias, systemic racism, microaggression, and racism in the media.

As library staff, we've all been on the receiving end of conversations with customers expressing their concerns about anything and everything. As a committee, we've created ways to bring multiple communities together that facilitate opportunities to address concerns, build relationships, create trust, and reinforce the library's position as a change agent. Although it's impossible to address everything, we can do our part by deeply and intentionally listening to our community members' concerns and by looking for recurring themes that we might be able to address as a system or with a collaborative relationship.

In the spirit of the fictional character Dr. Frasier Crane in the American television sitcoms *Cheers* and *Frasier,* let's all strive to adopt the approach of "I'm listening."

4

PARTNERING
FOR GREATER IMPACT

CINDY FESEMYER

Being an engaged information professional means that you collect community relationships in the same way your organization collects materials and information. Partnering makes for a more efficient, exponentially more creative, better connected, more-bang-for-your-buck library and a more vibrant community. Importantly, partnering also allows for shared risk.

Early on in my role as the director of a small, rural library in central Wisconsin, I was a solo cheerleader for my library and a solo cheerleader for the town. I was doing my job, but it wasn't fulfilling because I wasn't moving the needle on local knowledge or participation or community-building. A couple of years into my seven-year tenure at the Columbus Public Library, I found my people: the other local cheerleaders who wanted to make positive change in the community.

The relationship between three municipal departments—Columbus Recreation, the Columbus Area Senior Center, and the Columbus Public Library—blossomed over time. As trust grew, we planned large, community-wide events that one of us could never have pulled off alone.

Together we launched a new quarterly print magazine full of all the goings-on for the coming season. We joined efforts to address local health crises, including a high incidence of diabetes and an uptick in opioid use. We introduced each other to our networks and stood up for each other at meetings of municipal department heads. We became professional besties. We'd found our people.

Arianna Huffington described the value of partnership in a *Wall Street Journal* article about launching the *Huffington Post*:

> I had always worked on my own, but found you can do not just twice as much but 200 times as much when you have a good partner. It's this very creative connection. And having a partner definitely allows you to take more risks.[1]

Though the word *risk* is often associated with scary and dangerous behaviors like bungee jumping or drunk driving, there's more to it than mere thrill-seeking. Risk brings about creative change, rewarding courageous people for their hard work. If you want to be an agent of change in your profession, I urge you to take risks. And it's easier to take those risks when you're in good company.

APPROACHING A POTENTIAL PARTNER

The first important step in engaged partnering is to take that first step. There's no time like the present to literally get yourself out there to start exploring your options. This exploration begins the very important process of relationship building . . . and it is a process. In their *American Psychology* article "Building Community Resilience to Violent Extremism through Genuine Partnerships," researchers B. Heidi Ellis and Saida Abdi note "that the very *process* of building partnerships around a team can build social capital, and is as important as the *outcome* of having a team in place to prepare for disasters" [my emphasis].[2] The researchers were studying the problem of violent extremism and found "that social connection is at the heart of resilient communities and any strategy to increase community resilience must both harness and enhance existing social connections."[3] Though this topic is very specific, the researchers' findings can be widely applied. Building community partnerships takes time, and how you spend that time together may determine the strength of the partnership down the road. The process of getting to know a new potential partner is, itself, work. By slowly building trust, accountability, and an appreciation for each other, you'll be ready for that joint project down the road. But how to start?

Start with a first date. Like any unknown, it's good to start small. Start with coffee. You aren't investing much money in that cup of caffeine, and you aren't investing much of your time to imbibe it. If you learned about this potential new partner from someone else, it might be more comfortable to ask that person along as well. At the very least, that third person can do introductions and get the process started.

I suggest you go into that first coffee date with a notebook and pen and a list of starter questions. These initial questions are the equivalent of first date small talk, which might lead to a second date. Here's a scenario.

Hypothetically speaking, let's say you're new to employment with the undergraduate library on campus. You're the library's first ever community liaison librarian. Because the library has never had this position, administrators didn't give you much direction at the start. Begin by assessing current partnerships, but be sure to look beyond usual campus partners. In fact, look outside the campus altogether by exploring the whole community. Take a short field trip to find out what businesses are located close to campus and serve both community and campus populations. This is quickie community mapping and a good way to get in some extra steps on a workday. What businesses strike your fancy? A coffee shop? An art supply store? Then you find the perfect place. You're a board game geek, and you know that the board game store a block off campus holds regular gaming nights and that community and campus folks attend. Bingo!

You might start by taking the game store owner out for coffee and asking questions like these:

- Basic small talk:
    - Tell me about your business.
    - How long have you been there?
    - Why board games?
    - What are the best sellers at the store?

- Tell the owner about you:
    - You're new to your position in the academic library that serves undergrads.
    - You've seen the owner around the store the couple of times you've been in for game nights.
    - Yeah, you love the new expansion for that best-selling board game.

- Do your communities overlap? Ask:
    - Who are your typical customers?
    - Do you see many college students at your store?
    - Have you had good experiences with those college students?

There's more to the coffee date than asking your list of questions, though. Asking is the first step. Listening is the second. As the game store owner tells her story, don't think about what your next questions will be or fashion a board game pun for a quick retort. *Listen.* Really listen. This is a skill you need to develop in order to be an effectively engaged library professional. If your typical conversational style is to start speaking before the other person finishes or to have a response to everything everyone else says, don't do it. Fight that natural inclination. Get comfortable with a couple of ticks of silence. Show your respect for your potential partner by hearing them out completely. After you've listened, your next question or addition to the conversation will come naturally. You might find that you don't even need your list of questions if you can listen and respond to what you hear, conversationally and casually.

This coffee date is pure community engagement in action. First off, you left the library. You casually mapped your community on your short walk in the business district, taking note of where college students go and what kinds of stores are close to your library. You had a conversation with one of those business owners, one who would be easy for you to talk with. Even before meeting the owner, you knew you had shared interests: conversational gold. You already knew college students patronize the game store. This is pretty much a slam dunk for beginning the partnership process with your first community date. There's nothing wrong with relationships that come easily. In fact, these flawless first dates often lead to viable partnerships down the road. It's also a good idea to start your engagement efforts with a series of assured successes. You get an easy win or two and are comfortably practicing for the next possible first date. Easy first dates will build your confidence, and confidence is a key ingredient in the process of building engaged partnerships.

EASY PROJECTS WITH EASY PARTNERS

When the potential new relationship feels good, plan to do something together that won't cost much time or money. Start with something that's easy for your organization because it's only slightly different than what you do at the library every day. As an example, your first semester as the new community liaison librarian is coming to an end. It'll be time for exams in a few weeks. Your boss tells you to create some programs inside the library that will help students de-stress during this tense time of year. Your boss says the library did a few fun storytimes last year. The library partnered with the School of Education, and students came in to share storytime programs with a college twist. So there's already a partnership in place for you. Great. We'll get back to the School of Ed partnership shortly. In the meantime, why not kick it up a notch?

Let's pick up where we left off with the game store owner. Your first date was fun. You got a great recommendation for a new game, and the owner greeted you by name the next time you stopped in the shop. Why not look for a little more commitment from this potential partner?

Time to move on to lunch. Go prepared with an idea to pitch. As an example, you think it would be fun to host an exam week de-stress game-a-thon at the undergrad library. Turns out you have a perfect potential partner for that. Just like you did for your coffee date, prepare a list of questions ahead of time. Bring along that notebook and pen (screens are much too impersonal).

- Wanna try a small project together?
  - Are you interested in taking your show on the road?
  - How about hosting a midnight session of that new best-selling game at the undergrad library?
  - Yes, that game *is* pretty nerdy. I like your idea to add some mainstream games for people who need a break but aren't super board game nerds. What games do you recommend?
  - Old-school kid games sound great. How about one that gets them moving too? Do you have Twister to add to the mix?
  - Can you arrange to be there with me to see how things go? You can meet some potential new board gamers.
  - Sure, you're most welcome to bring coupons for the game store to share with the students.

You went into the conversation with an idea for a program. The game store owner augmented your idea with some of her own. You get to expand your programmatic offerings and bring a community business into your library. That business owner gets to see for herself whether the program works, and she gets to advertise her business at the local college. You both get something valuable out of the experience. This is the ideal outcome for any partnership but is especially important for a first time out. Consider this your first engagement liaison win. It was easy, right? Why not push yourself a little harder when the new semester begins?

WHAT DO YOU BRING TO THE TABLE? WHAT DO YOU NEED FROM A PARTNER?

Before you start the process of methodically searching for new partnerships, I urge you to think about yourself and your organization for a while first. Think of that data as an internal assessment of your organization. A typical way to analyze those traits in yourself and in your library is to work with others to identify organizational strengths, opportunities, aspirations, and results (SOAR). The Aspen Institute's *Action Guide for Re-Envisioning Your Public Library, Version 2.0* offers a version of a SOAR assessment (see the accompanying text box "SOAR

SOAR DEFINED

- **Strengths:** What does the library do very well now? What works? What are your assets and capabilities? What are your greatest strengths?
- **Opportunities:** Where in the current context are there opportunities for the library to make a difference, to contribute, to innovate? What are your best opportunities?
- **Aspirations:** What are your hopes and dreams for the future? What do you want to be known for? What is your preferred future?
- **Results:** What do you most want to accomplish? What will success look like?

Defined").[4] Using this tool, or the internal assessment tool of your choosing, is a good way to focus on where your organization is and where it wants to go.

You need to know yourself to know what kind of partner you need. Looking at the things you do well is a good start. This is what you bring to the table. For example, my library in Wisconsin brought to the partnership table a robust social media presence. We also brought the ability to operate outside the municipal Social Media Policy (a wonderful peculiarity of Chapter 43 of the Wisconsin Statutes).[5] So I could provide other municipal departments bound by the policy (e.g., Recreation and the Senior Center) very flexible social media marketing options. The library also employed a team of tech-savvy staff who could provide maximum social media marketing coverage. This was one of the strengths of my library as a potential partner.

On the other hand, though the library had more staff than either the Recreation Department or the Senior Center, most of them were tied to the library building most of the time. What we needed was people power, something the Recreation Department and Senior Center had plenty of. With directors who were as devoted to the community as we were, and a bevy of volunteers supporting their good works, they were just the partners we needed. They were happy to have us launch a new Facebook page to support the new local events publication, and we were happy to join their energetic volunteers in support of large-scale community events. Win-win. Even in the smallest towns in the most rural areas, there is someone to partner with. Even if there are few to no local businesses, perhaps there's a single individual who gets stuff done. Find that person!

Look at civic clubs, local schools, local businesses, faith organizations, health-care providers, law enforcement, nonprofit organizations, and other departments in your organization for what they bring to the table. Take note of what they might need that you can provide. Maybe a struggling Kiwanis Club (their mission is to support community literacy!) simply needs a new member. There's strength in joining local organizations and wearing your library hat when you attend meetings and functions. People might come to know you as a local mover and shaker yourself. What a compliment it would be if people with good ideas start at the library with questions about how to get started.

EXPANDING PARTNERSHIPS: MAPPING YOUR COMMUNITY

You need to figure out who you know in order to learn who you need to know. For example, you might have noticed a new influx of families at the library during the school day and learned that they're homeschool families. Your strong relationship with the local school will most likely show up on your community map, but maybe the homeschool families didn't. An adept and engaged library leader identifies trends within the library as reflections of the community it serves.

Whether you're looking for your first library partner, expanding your partnership pool with the addition of one or two new ones, or wanting to strengthen an already existing partnership, a good way to start digging deeper is to map your community. You can use an actual piece of paper that looks like the one in figure 4.1. It's a nice, visual way to prompt you to dig deep into your existing

FIGURE 4.1 | **Community map**

relationships, professional and personal. Perhaps you prefer a spreadsheet on your screen. I like this method too because you can start color-coding for types of relationships or relative strength of the relationship or whatever factors are important at the time. Or maybe you'd like to add partner names to a bunch of sticky notes and stick them under broad categories posted on the wall or a table. You can even color-code the sticky notes if that helps. This method is useful because you can move paper around as your thinking evolves. There are myriad ways to map your community. You're a librarian; you can find the right method for you and your organization.

Once you've found the perfect method to map your community, don't keep it to yourself. The true strength of this exercise comes with the addition of other people's maps. Perhaps a few other library staff people are equally interested in new partners. Or your library board or Friends of the Library is interested in exploring partnerships. Start with a few people you know you like to work with and try out your chosen community mapping tool with them. Do the mapping exercise together and pay attention to the overlapping relationships and the ones that stand alone on only one person's map. This is how you identify gaps in your organizational map. Perhaps other library staff people knew those homeschool families all along, but it never came up in conversation. And maybe you know the middle school librarian, and that other library staffer wants to introduce a tween book club but never gets away from the toddler set. Help each other by sharing the wealth of your community connections within your own organization.

When you're ready, you can take the tool one step farther by mapping with people out in the community, outside the walls of your library. Work with folks you know fairly well and see how your maps compare. Then take a chance and work with people you don't know well . . . yet. Mapping with different and diverse people will likely help you dig deeper into your own community relationships, remembering organizations you forgot about the first couple of times you mapped or finding some new ones you never knew about. With this information in hand, go back to the beginning and set up a coffee date with a new potential partner.

HOW TO REACT WHEN POTENTIAL PARTNERS APPROACH YOU

Let's say you've been the undergrad library's community liaison librarian for a couple of years and have developed a whole slate of great partners. Word will get out that you're a *promiscuous collaborator*. (This wonderful dating metaphor comes from Erica Freudenberger, a contributing author to this book.)

Believe me, being a promiscuous collaborator is a good thing. Eventually, people and organizations will start coming to you. You'll get e-mails or phone calls that start something like, "I noticed you hosted a dialogue series on immigration that brought together people from both the campus and the community." The caller will wonder if you might like to partner with him on another dialogue series, this one on building healthy habits for a happy life. Most of us are programmed to react negatively to a cold call. It's a symptom of living in a world of spam and robocalls. I urge you to fight that knee-jerk reaction. When people come to you, it's a sign that you're doing something right. Be open to new opportunities that expand your boundaries and your partnership potential.

As you listen to this new potential partner introduce himself, hearken back to how nervous you were a couple of years ago with the game store owner. Be generous in your assumptions and give the new person the benefit of the doubt. At the same time, start collecting information about this potential new partner. Did he come prepared? Is he listening closely when you answer his questions? Is conversation flowing naturally? Do you find yourself asking questions in return? Before you walk away from the café table, make sure you have next steps in place. Or not.

If you're not into it, that's important information too. If, despite your generous assumptions and benefit of the doubt, the person kind of offended you and wasn't really listening, it's okay to not follow up. Just shake hands and thank him for his time. If, on the other hand, you like what he had to say and you like how he said it and how he treated you, is it time for a lunch date? If so, mention it. Something like, "Hey, it was terrific meeting you and learning about your work. I see potential for a new community dialogue on the topic. How about you? Wanna get lunch sometime to start talking it through?"

One thing to look out for as you start exploring this new potential partner who came to you is how you might position your library with this relationship. Do you have the go-ahead to explore new activities, or are you bound by the new mission statement that calls for something this potential partner doesn't bring to the table? This is the cautionary part of partnerships. Explore constantly, and push boundaries along the way, but be careful to protect your organization and yourself. Overcommitment can lead to burnout. So make sure that all parties involved are equally pulling their own weight and that you don't end up with another half-time job when you work with this person or organization. That said, investigate scaling projects to match your library's mission and your available time. If the person or organization wants to start big, and if you like the idea and you like the partner, suggest starting small. In short, say *yes!* even if it means you must qualify that yes in order to get started with someone new.

INTRODUCE PARTNERS TO PARTNERS

The best way I've found to qualify a yes is to simply see how you can help that potential partner's efforts. Truly, the best thing you might be able to offer is a good listening ear and some thoughtful follow-up questions. People with big ideas often need to hear them out loud to start getting a grip on how to proceed. It's easy to be that sounding board. Beyond that, it's also pretty darn easy to offer to connect them with resources that will help them with their idea. That could be connecting them to more traditional library resources like data or materials. More likely, it's an introduction to other folks who might like to join the project. One of my favorite ways to say yes without overcommitting is a promise at the end of the call or meeting: "I will send a follow-up e-mail that introduces you to a couple of people who might like to help." Don't downplay the impact you can make in simply connecting people. Being a community connector is a powerful position for a library to occupy.

When you decide to fully commit to a new project with a new or evolving partner, but the project still seems too big for just the two of you, that's another great time to expand the circle and bring in one of your other community partners, or ask the new partner to bring in one of his, or do both. It's a good idea to find ways to collaborate with multiple community partners on very big projects that simply cannot happen without many hands and brains and hours. But the adage that many hands make light work can be deceiving. As a new project with new relationships gets under way, things might move a bit slowly in the beginning as partners get to know each other, exploring boundaries and personalities, to see how things fit. That's okay. The process of creating a good partnership takes work.

WEEDING PARTNERSHIPS

Sometimes things don't go as we've planned. As we know from simply living, things change, and things end. Invariably. Partnerships break up, sometimes due to disagreement, sometimes because the relationship simply runs its course. When it's time, it's okay to let partnerships go. Remember that we are collecting partners in the same way that we collect physical and electronic resources for our communities. Like those more traditional materials and resources, partnerships will invariably need to be weeded.

Over the course of a career, library professionals will participate in a wide variety of partnerships for many different reasons. How you acquire those partnerships will vary as well. You might have inherited existing partnerships when you took the job. Or been brought into an existing community partnership with two other organizations. Or created a partnership anew. Additionally, circumstances can change, causing you to reassess your partnerships. Budgets could be cut at either partner's organization. Community needs and aspirations might change. Staff change is virtually guaranteed at some point. Sometimes partnerships just take a turn toward dysfunction, and one or both sides are unhappy. These are all opportune times to reassess partnerships.

Changes in staff, demographics, or community trends can make it very difficult to continue with some partnerships. If a good partnership hasn't yet become an organizational bond and still depends on two specific people working well together, it can sometimes be tough to continue the relationship when one person leaves. If the community's history is as a predominantly Swiss community but hardly any Swiss people live there anymore, it could be difficult to find reasons to carry on with a Swiss heritage partner. If the community is suffering from the opioid epidemic and your library wants to tackle it but is full up, maybe a partnership that is floundering needs to be cut to make way for a new relationship with the local hospital as an opioid partner.

Despite all your best efforts, a professional relationship that used to flourish just might not be magical anymore. Bad relationships are hard. Oh, that there were a magic recipe for assessing or fixing or ending a partnership when things start to turn sour. Sadly, no. It's up to you and your library to logically take the right steps for your library and for the community. No matter what, dysfunctional partnerships are not effective partnerships. Just as that medical journal from 1975 or that book of racist fairy tales must be weeded from the collection, so too must that bad or nonrelevant partnership. I can't tell you how to do it, but I can recommend that you take a respectful and logical approach to the breakup.

The result of weeding is not tragic; it's glorious. Cutting away the old growth, making room for new. For some of us, it's an easy and natural process. For others it can be difficult, depending on how emotionally involved you are with the materials or resources or partners being weeded. Do your best to see the potential positive results of sunsetting a partnership as you disengage.

STRENGTHEN EXISTING PARTNERSHIPS

The meeting of two personalities is like the contact of two chemical substances: if there is any reaction, both are transformed.

—CARL GUSTAV JUNG[6]

Like Arianna Huffington and Carl Jung, our two researchers, B. Heidi Ellis and Saida Abdi, are talking about change when they talk about partnership. Positive change is at the core of good working partnerships. Over time, partners get to know each other more deeply, exploring both positive and negative aspects of the relationship. They also develop reputations within their communities as specialists in the area of that partnership and as team players.

Let's go back to the original partnership between the university undergrad library and the local game store. It's been five years of regular gaming in the library, with the game store becoming the presumed partner. You and the game store owner have a terrific friendship at this point, and your organizations have also bonded. Staff from both organizations know and trust each other and often plan programs without you at this point. It is taken for granted that there will be gaming in the undergrad library, and this tight organizational bond is a huge part of that presumption.

Throughout those five years, your library has occasionally held focus groups on community-university partnerships and has been actively surveying participants in all library programs. Results often point to your gaming partnership and program as an excellent example of a campus-community success story, and word is spreading across the campus and within the game store community. You learn the School of Education (a previous partner, remember?) is interested in gamification, a current trend in elementary education, and instructors want to give some School of Ed students hands-on, practical experience with the process. Can the undergrad library help? Or a local school, maybe? At the same time, other game store owners are asking your game store owner how they can get in on the partnership action. Throughout the semester multiple convenings of these stakeholders are held at your library, at the School of Ed, at the local elementary school, and at a new game store. Time spent listening to each other results in a memorandum of understanding for a pilot project to gamify a statewide fourth-grade state history unit next semester. The undergrad library, game store staff, and the School of Ed will team up on the project itself. Four different board game stores will hold play-demos of the project with students and teachers from the local elementary school to help School of Ed students refine the product. Win-win-win-win.

Nice result, huh?! Well, it all started with an idea and a coffee date. In my opinion, partnerships that begin casually like that are a good way to begin. Don't take things too seriously, and don't begin your exploration with a structure or rules before you even know if you can pull off a simple joint effort. Assuming you do pull it off and depending on the rules of the organizations involved in the partnership, some degree of formality might need to be introduced into the relationship at some point. If you learn that something more formal is required, that's when you need help. Consult your boss or municipality or legal department for assistance. Do your best to keep the paperwork as simple as possible while still fulfilling requirements. That will take the focus off the bureaucratic aspects of the partnership and keep it on the creative side of things, as it should be.

With good, time-tested partners, libraries and information agencies are pushing the boundaries of traditional librarianship. Libraries have blown past the walls of their buildings and are programming in all available spaces, providing services our communities need. With partners from hospitals to financial specialists, theaters to community centers, we're strutting our stuff all over town.

NOTES

1. Teri Evans, "Scrapping the Presses to Start HuffPo," *The Wall Street Journal*, May 25, 2010, https://www.wsj.com/articles/SB10001424052748704026204575266513147033900.

2. B. H. Ellis and S. Abdi, "Building Community Resilience to Violent Extremism through Genuine Partnerships," *American Psychologist* 72, no. 3 (April 2017): 293.

3. Ellis and Abdi, "Building Community Resilience," 289.

4. The Aspen Institute, *Action Guide for Re-Envisioning Your Public Library, Version 2.0* (Washington, DC: The Aspen Institute, 2017), 20, https://csreports.aspeninstitute.org/documents/ActionGuideFINAL_7_12_17.pdf.

5. Wisconsin State Legislature, "Chapter 43. Libraries," from *Updated 2017–18 Wisconsin Statutes and Annotations*, last modified January 3, 2020, https://docs.legis.wisconsin.gov/statutes/prefaces/toc.

6. Carl Gustav Jung, *Modern Man in Search of a Soul* (London: Kegan Paul, Trench, Trubner, 1933).

RESPECT AND COMPROMISE AID SCHOOL-CITY PARTNERSHIP

CINDY FESEMYER

A s instructional media center coordinator for the Zion-Benton Township High School in Zion Township, Illinois, Deborah Will partnered with the township supervisor's office to create a unique book club. She applied to be part of the American Library Association's Great Stories Club program, a reading and discussion model that trains library workers to lead book clubs about race and identity with underserved youth, particularly teens facing difficult life circumstances. In this case, Will would be working with a group of 14- to 16-year-olds who were employed with the township's summer work program.

Will used her professional connections and received training from the American Library Association (ALA) on facilitation and organizing; Zion Township Supervisor Cheri Neal worked her professional connections and created a paid summer intern position at City Hall. Deb worked a connection with a local woman who had marched with the late Congressman John Lewis and arranged for local kids to visit her nursing home to hear her stories firsthand after reading *March: Book One* by Lewis, Andrew Aydin, and Nate Powell. Cheri got local law enforcement, the mayor, and a city councilman on board for the book discussions.

The challenge arose when Neal read the books that the teens would be discussing. When she finished reading Angie Thomas's *The Hate U Give,* a novel about a teen girl who witnesses a white police officer shoot a Black boy, she was shocked. How could she ever condone the local high school's plan to build

SUCCESSFUL PARTNERSHIPS IN THREE STEPS

Deb and Cheri put their success down to these factors:

1. **Find common denominators:** study your community. What is everyone talking about? What aren't they talking about, but everyone knows? Discuss over coffee.

2. **Step up and step back:** focus on yes people. When soliciting new partners, look for those that respond "Yes!" Or, "yes, although . . . ," offering positive creativity. Beware of those whose every reply is "yes, but . . . ," offering excuses and roadblocks.

3. **Establish trust:** just say yes. When potential partners ask you for assistance, support them. They'll be more likely to support you when you ask for help in the future. Deb says, "Be a worker bee before you try to be a queen bee."

a community reading program that included this book? "Every other word is an F bomb!" she recalled.

Neal called up Will, her partner in this effort to address community racial equity issues. Will listened when Neal said that 14- and 15-year-olds couldn't handle the book. She listened when Neal talked about not backing this program anymore.

Will had two options for her reply:

1. Decry censorship and point to their signed memorandum of understanding for the program, or
2. Explain ALA's Freedom to Read statement and ask Cheri, "Do you want kids to read and watch it alone or with peers and mentors in the room?"

Needless to say, Will took the route of respect and empathy and did the latter. Their months of working together on the project taught them both to be present for each other and listen closely to what the other was saying, looking for common goals that focused on the big picture.

A councilman who attended the "Hate You Give" community program was so impressed that he personally financed tickets for all high school freshmen to attend the movie when it came out. English and social studies teachers created lessons to correspond with the trip to the movies. Many hands working together created conversations necessary for current and future work on issues of racial equality in their community.

COMMUNITY-CENTERED PROGRAMMING
Tools and Techniques

AUDREY BARBAKOFF

How do you plan programs and services *by* and *with,* rather than *for* or *at,* your community? At the King County Library System (KCLS), a fifty-branch system near Seattle, Washington, our move toward community-centered programming and services began with an effort to discover what residents considered their highest hopes, dreams, and plans for the future. The extensive feedback we received created a new Strategic Focus that fortifies KCLS as an organization that emphasizes teamwork, setting priorities and strategic goals, and building on staff strengths. It reflects the library system's commitment to public service and accountability as well as our deep intention to enhance lives, forge connections, and strengthen communities.

Like many libraries across the country, KCLS was already supporting vibrant local economies and personal financial success in myriad ways: job and business events, databases for career information and skills, financial literacy classes, and more. However, with the addition of a community engagement and economic development manager position to the staff, the library saw an opportunity to develop a more impactful and responsive unified vision for these efforts. The result was the Economic Empowerment Framework, a plan for developing programs and services in this topic area. The framework was developed with extensive input and engagement from the community, and it taught us how to create economic empowerment services with the community at the heart.

In the process of developing the framework, KCLS utilized a variety of methods to engage its community. The processes, in both strategic planning and service development, could be applied to any subject area or even an over-all service assessment. This chapter provides an overview of the community engagement process that led to the overall strategy. We will then explore the practical application of that strategy by describing a community-led event, Negocios Redondos / We Mean Business!, that was developed as a result. Finally, we will take a deeper dive into evaluating success, for both a broad strategy and a specific event. By the end of the chapter, you should understand how to engage the community in developing a service plan, apply that strategy to create a community-led program, and evaluate success.

GETTING STARTED: DEVELOPING THE COMMUNITY ENGAGEMENT PLAN

The foundation for successful, meaningful community engagement is a clear understanding of what the library is hoping to achieve and why. A general "community engagement" process that is not tethered to a specific goal may result in confusion and frustration for the library and its partners because people will not understand how the information gathered will be used to make a difference. In the case of KCLS's Economic Empowerment Framework, our purpose was to offer staff a shared focus for making decisions about services and programs. In a large system, this shared focus allows staff in individual libraries to make local decisions that still align with what other libraries are doing and that contribute to a collective, system-wide impact. However, a system of any size will benefit from a shared understanding of what is most important.

KCLS began by developing a framework, rather than simply diving into planning community-led individual programs, to achieve the greatest impact with our resources. All public libraries serve many constituencies and must balance competing priorities for limited staff time and funds. By trying to do too much for too broad an audience, a library could find itself providing scattershot, one-off services that do not make a deep enough impact, or it might invest in a coordinated, sustained effort that is not aligned with what the community truly wants. By contrast, with a clear, evidence-based focus developed in partnership with the community, the library can use the same set of resources to confidently focus on aligned actions that cumulatively make a meaningful difference.

Community engagement also ensures that the library's strategies and pro-grams uphold the profession's core value of diversity.[1] Library staff, especially MLIS-degreed librarians, often do not fully reflect the diverse demographics of the community.[2] Even in libraries with a diverse staff, any individual librarian will likely not belong to most of the communities she serves. In order to understand the aspirations and challenges of diverse communities and engage their many strengths and assets, library staff must dialogue with them directly.

For any library to design truly inclusive services for a community, those services must be built with and by that community. Without diverse communities' engagement and support, staff run the risk of creating services that do not adequately support people's real goals, do not reach the intended audience effectively, lack cultural competence or relevance, unintentionally adopt a deficit-based perspective rather than an asset-based one, or produce any combination of these outcomes. The library may miss out on the opportunity to learn from, and grow alongside, powerful work already being done by members of underrepresented communities. The importance of this approach is summed up neatly by the popular activist maxim "nothing about us without us is for us."

COMMUNITY ENGAGEMENT TOOLS AND TECHNIQUES

A community engagement mindset begins by centering the community, not the library. In traditional planning, a library might begin by thinking about its existing services or what new ones it might develop. However, this approach tends to narrowly frame learning about the community through the lens of the institution's needs, goals, and existing processes. As a result, the library can miss out on identifying important stakeholders, seeing an accurate bigger picture of the community's aspirations and needs, and developing significant innovations. For an authentic understanding of the community, and to be able to engage effectively with community members in subsequent steps, libraries must learn to flip the process and make the community the lens through which library services will later be assessed. This strategy means focusing on deepening our understanding of the community first before attempting to make a direct connection to library services.

In developing the Economic Empowerment Framework, the KCLS steering committee engaged the community in multiple ways. This mix allowed us to gather different types of information and learn from a wide set of stakeholders. The primary methods we used to connect with our external community were environmental scanning, asset mapping, and key stakeholder interviews. For the internal community of staff, we employed online surveys, SOAR (strengths, opportunities, aspirations, and results) assessments with focus groups, and racial equity analysis. Many of the internal and external processes ran simultaneously; one important exception is that we intentionally began the project by focusing only on understanding the external community, without considering its relationship to library services.

External Engagement Tools

Environmental scans. Environmental scanning refers to the process of tracking current and emerging trends that are likely to impact a project's or an organization's success.[3] It generally considers both internal and external forces, though this section will focus specifically on external assessment. Environmental scans can take many forms, and various specific tools are available, but the trend-tracking goal can be achieved without any one particular methodology.

For this project, we needed to scan the environment to determine what factors were influencing economic development in our community. We started by identifying the key documents that described and guided big-picture planning for the region. Examples included the Workforce Development Council (WDC) of Seattle-King County's *2016–2020 Workforce Development Plan*, city/municipal growth plans, locally produced industry studies, and economic information released by area universities and colleges.

This research provided important background that informed how the committee chose to structure the rest of our discovery process. Most notably, we saw that the way our community categorizes economic development is significantly different from the way library staff had been considering it. As in many libraries, we generally divided up our audience by type of activity: job seekers, entrepreneurs, adult learners, and so on. However, our community planned in terms of sectors, such as health care or construction, each of which contained all activity types. This disparity resulted in a disconnect—although the library might previously have tried to serve "entrepreneurs" as a single audience, the business community might perceive major distinctions between an entrepreneur in health care and one in construction.

To better align with the community's self-perception, the committee reorganized the rest of our engagement work around specific sectors. We adopted four sectors of focus, based on those the WDC had already determined were currently the most salient in our region: health care, construction, manufacturing, and creative economy.[4] For each sector, a pair of staff members conducted a deep dive into its local organizations and documents to better understand its landscape. Each pair then distilled their key findings into a single page to share with the rest of the organization.

Asset maps. Our next step was to create asset maps for each sector. Asset maps are visual representations of the key players, resources, and relationships in a particular geographic or topical area.[5] They may be literal maps or conceptual diagrams. We employed conceptual mapping because our purpose was to produce insight into the constellation of connections in each sector regardless of geography, though each team varied its format to best represent its sector's unique ecosystem (figure 6.1). The final asset maps were paired

FIGURE 6.1 | **CREATIVE ECONOMY ASSET MAP**

Creative Economy Asset Map

Creative Economy (CE) is trade at the confluence of arts, culture, business, education, and technology. This Asset Map depicts relationships between community assets that support Creative Economy development in King County.

Spaces

- The Internet
- Libraries (Maker Spaces)
- Parks
- Performing Arts Centers
- Community Centers
- Schools
- Farmer's Markets
- Fairs
- Music Venues/Festivals
- Convention Center
- Seattle Center
- Media space (TV, radio, online, print)

These types of Spaces hold these Community Institutions

Community Institutions

- King County Library System
- Arts Corps
- Path with Art
- Small Business Administration
- Local Chambers of Commerce
- Libraries/Schools/Colleges
- WA State Arts Commission
- The Vera Project
- WorkSource
- 4 Culture
- Arts Ed Washington
- Public Health (food business)
- Shunpike
- Washington Technology Industry Association
- SCORE
- Apprenti
- Adobe Education Exchange

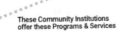

These Community Institutions offer these Programs & Services

Programs & Services

- Idea X
- Tech Tutor
- HS 21+
- Mentorship
- Apprenticeship
- Arts Education
- Software Certifications
- Job Clubs
- Financial Literacy
- Workshops
- Creative Consultancies
- Volunteerism
- Grants
- Festál

These Programs & Services are provided to these Audiences

Audiences

- Jobseekers And Employees (education, opportunities)
- Small Businesses And Nonprofits (networking, Marketing, Education on Business Plans, Licensing, Finances, Funding, etc.)
- Large Businesses (skilled workers, transportation, education/certification, infrastructure)
- Youth (social-emotional support and development, training and education, employment, internship/fellowship, affordable and adequate housing, medical care, transportation)

with their one-page descriptive narrative to produce a brief, simple, yet rich picture of each sector.

Key stakeholder interviews. At this point, committee members were ready to engage directly with the community. Because of our prior work, we were able to do this in a way that was both inclusive and strategic. We already understood what we wanted to achieve and who some of the key players were. Therefore, we could make intentional decisions about whose voices we needed to prioritize hearing. From creating our asset maps, we knew who the major stakeholders were in each industry and how they connected to each other. Because we had "done our homework" by reading relevant documents, we had the context to ask meaningful questions that respected our interviewees' time and expertise. We proactively sought out interviewees connected to economically marginalized communities to ensure that our recommendations would authentically serve those communities.

The staff who had researched each sector took the lead in identifying and contacting people from that industry to interview. In most cases, we did not have prior connections to the individuals and organizations we wished to engage. However, because we were able to clearly and succinctly describe our purpose in reaching out and demonstrate an understanding of what that particular person had to offer to the discussion, our cold calls generally received extremely warm receptions. Ultimately, we met with approximately thirty key stakeholders for one-on-one discussions.

We structured our interactions as informal discussions rather than formal interviews. Although we had a general outline of the kinds of information we wanted to learn, we focused more on authentically listening and building relationships than on asking a standardized set of questions. We chose this approach because obtaining information was only half the purpose of the conversations. The second, equally important goal was to build relationships. True engagement is not just about transfer of data but about creating deep, lasting involvement by sharing power and ownership. We intended these not to be one-time dialogues, but the first in an ongoing engagement process that might result in future collaborations.

As with the rest of the community discovery process, we framed the discussion around community aspirations and challenges rather than around library services. Therefore, our first questions often included questions such as these: What are your hopes or aspirations for your community? What are the most important challenges or gaps you are facing? What do you think should happen to get where you want to go? Only after this broad discussion did we try to contextualize together what an interviewee's responses might mean for library services. We often concluded conversations by asking, "Who else should I be talking with?" This question is powerful because one of the most effective ways to engage with parts of the community we have not previously reached is through personal introductions and word-of-mouth connections.

Following each discussion, the interviewer uploaded notes to a shared internal workspace for the rest of the committee to view. When the period in which we were conducting interviews was over, we reviewed all the notes to scan for important themes. The nuanced input we received heavily informed the final recommendations of the framework. Furthermore, before the framework was complete, we returned to a few of our interviewees to ask for their review of the draft recommendations. Although our process was not scientific or academic, this communication loop helped validate our conclusions.

Internal Engagement Tools

In any size library, the success of a community engagement project will depend on some amount of buy-in from the internal community of staff. The techniques for conducting internal community engagement play an important role in ultimately creating a sustainable community-led service or mindset. In general, what matters for staff buy-in is regular communication that focuses on why community-led work is important.

Online surveys. Because this project took place in the context of a large staff spread across many locations, we first conducted an online survey. As part of the environmental scan, we asked staff to describe what was currently happening in their libraries in regard to economic empowerment.

SOAR analysis with focus groups. We then took the broad themes from the survey to determine the audience and questions for several focus groups. We asked these groups to participate in a SOAR assessment (strengths, opportunities, aspirations, results).[6] SOAR functions similarly to the better-known SWOT analysis (strengths, weaknesses, opportunities, threats) but takes an asset-based approach by exchanging a focus on weaknesses and threats for one on aspirations and results (see the text box "SOAR Defined" in chapter 4). This model was also valuable because its additional two categories provided data about desired outcomes and metrics, which would later be essential in developing evaluation standards.

Racial equity assessment. Both an internal and external process, racial equity assessment allowed us to pause before finalizing our recommendations in order to systematically consider their potential impacts on vulnerable and marginalized communities. For a process to truly center all the community, not just the dominant culture, it must recognize the reality of structural and institutional racism and acknowledge that our services will, therefore, impact people in different ways. We must hold ourselves accountable for seeing and addressing those disparate impacts. That will mean focusing on what works for each community (equity) rather than on creating a single solution for everyone (equality). In community-led work, one size does not fit all.

To determine where our work might have disparate or unintended negative impacts, the Economic Empowerment team utilized the Racial Equity Toolkit created by the Seattle Race and Social Justice Initiative.[7] Because centering the community is essential in equity work, the first few steps of the toolkit closely mirror the inclusive process of learning and listening. The next phase was to determine benefit and burden. In short, who specifically will be impacted by what we propose, and how might those recommendations help or harm them? Once that is understood, how might we amplify the benefits and mitigate the possible harms? Finally, how will we hold ourselves accountable for more equitable results and continue to communicate with impacted communities about how we can improve?

A single conversation or process concerning racial equity will not solve every problem related to systemic racism, especially when members of the impacted community are not present. However, it may be surprising how many issues can be surfaced quickly with even a small amount of focused conversation, and how some small changes can lead to big impact. Although it is important for equity work to be ongoing, it is also crucial that we do not feel so overwhelmed by the enormity of the problem that we do not start at all. Building even a short racial equity assessment into a community-centered planning process can begin to normalize these discussions.

One Size Does Not Fit All

KCLS found the preceding internal and external engagement techniques to be effective for its context and community, but there are many other possible tools for substantive community engagement. Libraries should select methods based on their own goals and local context.

For example, this project committee selected individual interviews rather than focus groups with community members, largely because we found that key stakeholders in the business community faced high scheduling constraints. We did not conduct a large-scale online or written public survey because this tool was being used by the system for other purposes. However, these approaches might be the right fit in other communities.

Consider the ultimate goal, then determine which method(s) might best contribute to reaching that goal in your particular community and library. What really matters is not the tool selected but that the library develop a process that meaningfully engages and centers community.

The Results

As a result of this community engagement process, KCLS's Economic Empowerment committee recommended focusing on eight specific audiences (for example, entrepreneurs who are immigrants and refugees, and new adults without a four-year degree).

For each audience, we provided a one-page Lean Canvas that identified key economic opportunities and needs, types of library service responses, ways to evaluate success, and effective communication channels and messaging.[8] These recommendations, along with the sector environmental scans, asset maps, and de-identified aggregate survey, interview, and focus group results, were assembled into the final Economic Empowerment Framework.

NEGOCIOS REDONDOS / WE MEAN BUSINESS!

The purpose of developing a framework is not simply to have it done; it is to guide action. The first service we undertook as a direct result of the Economic Empowerment Framework, and used as a pilot to test the conclusions, was a Latinx entrepreneur fair entitled Negocios Redondos / We Mean Business!

We selected the general topic and direction of the program because it served an audience of focus identified in the framework—specifically, immigrant and refugee entrepreneurs. In some areas of our community, a large portion of this population is Hispanic and monolingual or bilingual Spanish-speaking. One of the clear lessons from our engagement during the framework development was that in this community, economic empowerment services needed to be provided in culturally relevant ways. Therefore, we decided to make the event not simply informational but celebratory and community-building as well.

At that point, we stopped our own planning and engaged our partners. The mindset shift we had undergone during the framework development process taught us to not simply invite our focus audiences to the table but to build the table together. We called about a dozen contacts from within the Latinx entrepreneur community, many of them initially made or strengthened during the key stakeholder interview process. We laid out the bare bones—an event for Latinx entrepreneurs that also celebrated Hispanic Heritage Month—and asked what they thought such an event should look like and if they'd be willing to help make it happen.

As a result, the event took shape in a very different way than it might have if library staff had planned it alone based on our own knowledge and assumptions about the community. Some differences were small, such as using the term *Latinx* rather than *Hispanic* and holding the event on Saturday rather than Sunday. Other changes were a dramatic departure from our usual practices, such as actively encouraging families to attend together and providing children's activities in the same room as the adult program.

From our partners, we learned that although Latinx entrepreneurs wanted to learn about services and resources, they wanted even more to hear from successful business owners in their own community. This realization led to an entrepreneur success story panel. We also learned that people were looking for opportunities to grow their marketing skills and were sometimes uncomfortable promoting their products. Responding to this information, we offered elevator pitch practice. Armed with this kind of information and engagement, library staff were able to focus our resources not on developing our own ideas but on supporting and enabling the vision of the partners from within the community.

Ultimately, the event included a panel of successful Latinx entrepreneurs sharing their stories, paired with service providers who supported them along the way; a resource fair with Spanish-language and bilingual service providers; elevator pitch practice; networking time, with refreshments provided by a local Latinx-owned business; and a children's activity (making Mexican folk art sculptures called *alebrijes*). Because the many highly engaged partners reached out to invite their own networks, we had a turnout of more than fifty entrepreneurs from sixteen different zip codes, primarily Latinx women whose preferred language was Spanish.

In planning this program, library staff shifted our role from leader to facilitator, from holding power to sharing power. Changing perspectives in this way is fundamentally equity work. In a community-led program, librarians give up our role as gatekeepers and final decision-makers. Instead, we turn our resources and power over to the community of people we want to engage, supporting them as they create the reality they wish to see. We move away from a traditional planning model of informing or consulting to one of full collaboration and empowerment.[9] In making this change, we shift away from a deficit-based model that treats vulnerable communities as victims in need of help and into an asset-based model whereby we approach those communities with deep respect for their many strengths and abilities. In this mindset, the library focuses on providing a community with the support and resources that it has been systematically denied, so that it has an opportunity to serve itself and others.

EVALUATION

Taking the time to evaluate the results of a community-led initiative is essential to the process. The purpose of this evaluation is not to accumulate data for its own sake or to achieve a specific numerical benchmark. Instead, the purpose is relational. The library owes it to our partners and community to understand whether we are truly serving them in a meaningful way and to determine how we can continue to improve and grow. These goals mean that libraries need to create space for our partners, program participants, and staff to reflect on their experience and share their insight. Doing so both deepens our relationships and promotes continuous service improvement.

Even understanding the value of evaluation in community engagement work, staff may be hesitant if they do not know how to conduct it. When an overall strategy or a specific program is community-led, how can the library evaluate success? Different communities will invariably want and need unique outcomes, and traditionally underrepresented groups will most likely value aspects outside the standard metrics libraries often collect. Therefore, a standard one-size-fits-all measurement is unlikely to truly provide insight into whether a strategy or program was successful, to what extent, and why.

The key to successful evaluation is to treat it as an integral part of the planning process from the very beginning, not as something additional that happens at the end. It starts when the stakeholders develop an understanding of the intended impact of the program, service, or strategy. Gaining an understanding of what outcomes actually matter to community members requires close engagement with them.

For the Economic Empowerment Framework, we turned to our key stakeholder interview notes to understand desired impacts. For each focus audience, active members of that community had told us what was important to them, what they aspired to for the future, and what they thought needed to happen or change to get there. The staff committee distilled those responses into a set of measurable changes in knowledge, skill, ability, feeling, or status. For example, for entrepreneurs who are immigrants and refugees, key outcomes included the following: participants report increased awareness of factors affecting their business and ways in which to navigate those factors; users demonstrate feeling safe and welcome by actively engaging during programs, by using services repeatedly, or by doing both; and participants report that they have identified and taken action toward their business goal. Before finalizing these evaluation standards, we brought them back to the interviewees to see if the general outcomes statements aligned with their own visions of success.

When developing a specific program, such as Negocios Redondos / We Mean Business!, the organizers began by referring back to these evaluation standards in the framework. Although not every metric in the framework was meant to be equally relevant in every situation, it provided a starting point and guideline for identifying important outcomes for this particular program. Based on those outcomes, library staff could then determine the best methods to use for measuring or evaluating them.

In this instance, my organization was fortunate to be able to hire a graduate student to support the development of the evaluation methodology. Katya Yefimova, a PhD student at the University of Washington iSchool, designed a survey for program participants that would help assess how effectively we had reached our focus audience and which aspects of the program were most and least valuable in achieving the intended outcomes. She also observed the program, took notes, and guided staff through conducting brief interviews with program attendees. Finally, she synthesized these results into conclusions and recommendations.

Although this type of expert outside support is a rarity, its lessons provided a foundation that will be useful in ongoing evaluation work by staff. One primary takeaway was to reinforce the value of evaluation methods other than formal surveys. Although we did provide a paper survey, just as much or more of our assessment came from other sources: ideas from previous stakeholder interviews and SOAR assessments; brief, casual, one-on-one conversations with participants about why they attended and whether their goals were met; and observations of the room to see who felt safe enough to ask questions or speak up, which activities were popular, and how people interacted. When the librarian has a clear picture of the program's ideal impact, impeccable survey design or perfectly standardized interactions are significantly less important than making the effort to listen deeply to participants and stakeholders—in whatever way works best for all involved.

From the very first time the Economic Empowerment committee read a document or interviewed a stakeholder, and long before any discussion of statistics or metrics, its members were thinking about and engaging in evaluation. In the early phases of developing the framework, we painted a clear picture of success by engaging with community members to understand what kind of future they wanted to achieve. Later, after we had identified the groups we would focus on and worked with them to determine the library's direction, we discussed how we would know whether, to what extent, and in what ways we were making the difference we intended. This overarching strategic work then guided the planning process for a specific program, which also retained the flexibility to respond to the specific needs of that individual circumstance and group of participants. What we might normally think of as "evaluation"— the surveys and other techniques employed on the day of the event, and their debrief afterward—were the last, rather than the first or only, steps.

The evaluation process is circular rather than linear. The new understanding gained from our evaluation of Negocios Redondos / We Mean Business! should lead to new or improved services, which will then be evaluated themselves. Ultimately, though many methods of evaluation are available, and having some standardized metrics such as attendance or user satisfaction can be a helpful reporting tool, much of the true work of evaluation is about building a culture in which goals are developed in partnership with the community and everyone takes time for reflection during and after.

USING COMMUNITY ENGAGEMENT TOOLS TO DEVELOP PROGRAM STRATEGY

KCLS used community engagement tools to develop a strategy for a program area, created a community-led program based on that strategy, and evaluated both. Although the Economic Empowerment Framework was a specific project, the mindset and techniques it used to center community can be adapted for and applied in many situations and types of libraries. Describing one specific community-led program based on the framework, Negocios Redondos / We Mean Business!, provided a concrete example of how to translate an abstract strategy into a service for patrons. Finally, a discussion of evaluation revealed that though many specific metrics and techniques are available, the core of the work is engaging with impacted communities to develop a clear, shared vision of success and taking the time to listen deeply to understand whether, in what ways, and why that vision was achieved. Evaluation can be used to improve both the relationship and future services. Ultimately, community engagement matters because its inherently asset-based approach leads to services and relationships that promote equity, diversity, and inclusion in the community.

NOTES

1. "Core Values of Librarianship," American Library Association, adopted January 2019, www.ala.org/advocacy/intfreedom/corevalues.

2. American Library Association, *Diversity Counts* (Chicago: American Library Association, 2007), www.ala.org/aboutala/sites/ala.org.aboutala/files/content/diversity/diversitycounts/diversitycounts_rev0.pdf.

3. "Conducting an Environmental Scan," Fordham University, https://www.fordham.edu/info/26625/conducting_an_environmental_scan.

4. Workforce Development Council of Seattle-King County, *2016–2020 Seattle-King County Workforce Development Plan*, 2016, https://static1.squarespace.com/static/53c04ba6e4b0012ad48d079e/t/58923d9529687fda177bf36b/1485979039718/2016-2020+Seattle-King+County+Local+Workforce+Development+Plan_FINAL+7.27.2016.pdf.

5. "Community Toolbox," Center for Community Health and Development at the University of Kansas, https://ctb.ku.edu/en.

6. The Aspen Institute, *Action Guide for Re-Envisioning Your Public Library, Version 2.0* (Washington, DC: The Aspen Institute, 2017), https://csreports.aspeninstitute.org/documents/ActionGuideFINAL_7_12_17.pdf.

7. "Racial Equity Toolkit to Assess Policies, Initiatives, Programs, and Budget Issues," Seattle Race and Social Justice Initiative, 2012, https://www.seattle.gov/Documents/Departments/RSJI/RacialEquityToolkit_FINAL_August2012.pdf.

8. Ash Maurya, "Capture Your Business Model in 20 Minutes," YouTube, January 23, 2013, video, 22:59, https://www.youtube.com/watch?v=7o8uYdUaFR4.

9. "IAP2 Spectrum of Public Participation," IAP2: International Association for Public Participation, 2018, https://cdn.ymaws.com/www.iap2.org/resource/resmgr/pillars/Spectrum_8.5x11_Print.pdf.

ETHICAL AND INCLUSIVE COMMUNITY ENGAGEMENT

ELLEN KNUTSON *and* QUANETTA BATTS

E
thics and inclusion should be at the center of all your community engagement programs. Unfortunately, good intentions—even the best intentions—do not automatically lead to fair and equitable outcomes. We all have implicit bias and un- or underexamined privilege. Although library and information science professional ethics and core values are strong in the area of inclusion, putting these ideas into practice can sometimes be challenging because of organizational inertia and a small appetite for risk.[1] By carefully considering the potential impacts of your actions and plans, you will be on your way to providing truly ethical and inclusive engagement programs.

This chapter will look at how libraries have focused on ethics and inclusion in their community engagement work and how that focus has strengthened their community relationships. We will pull from our personal experiences—Quanetta Batts from her work at The Ohio State University Libraries, and Ellen Knutson from her work with library workers who have gone through Kettering Foundation library research exchanges—as well as from the experiences of other librarians. We will discuss power and privilege, point out some ways that library workers can be intentional in their practice, and talk about the importance of relationship-building for any library worker or library system that hopes to provide ethical and inclusive community engagement. But first, we look closer at some core principles of community engagement.

CORE PRINCIPLES OF COMMUNITY ENGAGEMENT

An organization's community engagement work can be thought of as a spectrum of its interactivity with the community. On one end, you see organizations that are more insular in their public participation, serving mainly as providers of information. At the other extreme, you see organizations that are fully collaborative and democratic, relinquishing a great deal of decision-making and control. This range is outlined in the spectrum of public participation created by the International Association for Public Participation (IAP2).[2] (See figure 1.1.)

The Vancouver Public Library in British Columbia, Canada, was one of the pioneers to apply a community engagement continuum to library work through the Working Together Project. The project developed a public involvement continuum (figure 7.1) to illustrate the ranges of engagement in library services.[3]

FIGURE 7.1 | **PUBLIC INVOLVEMENT CONTINUUM**

PUBLIC INVOLVEMENT CONTINUUM				
GIVING INFORMATION	GETTING INFORMATION		ENGAGING	PARTNERING/ COLLABORATING
INFORM/ EDUCATE ↓	CONSULT ↓	DISCUSS/ DEBATE ↓	ENGAGE/ PARTICIPATE ↓	PARTNER/ COLLABORATE ↓
Library plans services and informs the public of the services.	Library asks the community what it wants or finds important.	Library asks the community what it wants or finds important.	Library involves community in library activities.	Library works with community members to plan services.
OUTREACH	SURVEYS	FOCUS GROUPS	ADVISORY COMMITTEES	COLLABORATIVE
LIBRARY BOOTHS	POLLS	PUBLIC MEETINGS		SERVICE
MARKETING	OVER-THE-DESK CHATS	SEMINARS	EXPERT ADVISORS	DEVELOPMENT
ICT TRAINING			COMMUNITY PANELS	
LITERACY PROMOTION	FEEDBACK FORMS			COMMUNITY-LED SERVICE PLANNING
PRESS & PAMPHLETS				
OPEN HOUSES				

LISTENING
CONSULTING
ENGAGING
COLLABORATING

On the left side of the continuum, the library is centered, and librarians make decisions about what the community needs and how to meet those needs. As you move across the continuum to the right, the community has more and more impact on decisions about every aspect of library service delivery. At the far right, the community is leading the service planning. (It is important to note that this continuum is not about the quality of the program but about the depth of the engagement.)

The National Coalition for Dialogue and Deliberation (NCDD) convened a group of public participation leaders to outline the core principles of public engagement. Librarians who follow these principles in their community engagement work will be toward the collaborating side of the engagement spectrum.

NCDD and its collaborators developed seven core principles of public engagement:

1. *Careful planning and preparation*: Through adequate and inclusive planning, ensure that the design, organization, and convening of the process serve both a clearly defined purpose and the needs of the participants.
2. *Inclusion and demographic diversity*: Equitably incorporate diverse people, voices, ideas, and information to lay the groundwork for quality outcomes and democratic legitimacy.
3. *Collaboration and shared purpose*: Support and encourage participants, government and community institutions, and others to work together to advance the common good.
4. *Openness and learning*: Help all involved listen to each other, explore new ideas unconstrained by predetermined outcomes, learn and apply information in ways that generate new options, and rigorously evaluate public engagement activities for effectiveness.
5. *Transparency and trust*: Be clear and open about the process, and provide a public record of the organizers, sponsors, outcomes, and range of views and ideas expressed.
6. *Impact and action*: Ensure each participatory effort has real potential to make a difference, and that participants are aware of that potential.
7. *Sustained engagement and participatory culture*: Promote a culture of participation with programs and institutions that support ongoing quality public engagement.[4]

Following these principles will help ensure quality engagement, and to this we add the lens of equity and inclusion, encouraging you to both deepen your engagement and increase the equity of your community engagement work.

We think that it is important to center inclusion at each point, weighing which actions are opening opportunities for all people in your community, and to ask questions that start to peel back layers of privilege that may cloud our vision.

The intersection of equity and engagement can be mapped as a quadrant:

Reducing barriers in the library, such as eliminating fines or strict proof of address requirements, increases equity in the library but requires little engagement with the community to accomplish.

High Equity

Collaborating with low-income caregivers on how best to increase kindergarten readiness and implementing their recommendations in the library's programming require high engagement and will increase equity.

Low Engagement

High Engagement

An author talk with Q&A planned by library staff with little input from the community does not require much engagement and does not increase equity unless additional equity work is included.

Low Equity

Strong collaboration with a local gardening group that is overwhelmingly white and middle class, or in a branch that has high food security, to develop programming related to gardening and local food may be high on the engagement spectrum but may not increase equity unless additional equity measures are included.

Using both theory and examples from libraries, we will examine issues that affect equity and offer tools and suggestions for increasing equity and deepening engagement with your community.

UNDERSTANDING POWER AND PRIVILEGE

If you are reading this book, you have power and privilege. You have the privilege of literacy and the privilege of understanding English, one of the major global languages. Because this book is written for library workers, you likely have the privilege of education, and, statistically speaking, you are likely to possess white privilege.[5]

In her seminal work, feminist and anti-racism activist Peggy McIntosh outlines the "invisible knapsack" of white privilege. She lists fifty conditions that illustrate the daily effects of white privilege in her life, including these: "26. I can easily buy posters, post-cards, picture books, greeting cards, dolls, toys and children's magazines featuring people of my race." And "39. I can be late to a meeting without having the lateness reflect on my race."[6] As you plan and prepare for your engagement programs, we recommend taking a look at McIntosh's article and working with your team on identifying your privilege. Although McIntosh focuses on white privilege, the questions and statements are easily modified for thinking about other kinds of privilege as well (age, ability, sexual orientation, gender, and others).

Librarian John Berry adapted some of McIntosh's statements to specifically apply to library settings—for example, "8. When conducting collection development, I can easily find materials featuring people of my race." And "10. I can criticize my library or my profession and talk about how much I fear its policies and behavior without being seen as an outsider."[7] Berry wrote these statements as a way to help librarians think beyond the idea that respecting and achieving diversity is as simple as treating everyone with kindness. Kindness should certainly be encouraged, but it falls short when you don't take into consideration the privilege and power that exist in a given situation.

This kind of self-reflection is important. In *Information Services to Diverse Populations: Developing Culturally Competent Library Professionals*, Nicole A. Cooke reminds us that

> [staff] should be aware of differences that may exist between themselves and the people they are serving. Patrons from diverse groups may have a variety of visible and invisible differences (or perhaps barriers) that could require extra attention, different resources, intercultural understanding, empathy, and so on. Diverse patrons can be perceived as "others" (as they may be perceived in society at large), and that could influence their approach [to] and usage of the library and its services. This hesitancy is above and beyond the library anxiety that many library users (and nonusers) experience. It becomes that much more crucial that the library staff strives to make all patrons feel at ease, and that patrons are welcomed and can be assisted.[8]

By identifying the privileges you have and how we as a society have developed notions of what is "normal" and "not normal," you will be on your way to understanding how implicit bias is formed and will start to recognize the blinders that limit our understanding of the world and the experiences of others. These blinders may influence who we include in our engagement programs and planning, or put up unintentional barriers that exclude some members of the community. For example, being monolingual (working only in English) will exclude those who do not speak English. Portland, Oregon's Multnomah County Library has instituted a "We Speak Your Language" project to overcome this barrier. The library provides services in six languages: English, Spanish, Chinese, Russian, Vietnamese, and Somali.[9]

Kimberlé Crenshaw's work will help you understand how the various components of identity intersect and the different levels of oppression or diminishment a person might feel. In "Mapping the Margins," Crenshaw coined the term *intersectionality,* which challenges us to understand the ways race, gender, age, economic status, and other identity markers make up these different levels of oppression.[10]

In a 2017 interview celebrating twenty years of racial justice work through the African American Policy Forum (AAPF) led by Crenshaw, she discussed the ways power comes and collides. She encouraged us not to think of different "isms" as separate issues. "It's not simply that there's a race problem here, a gender problem here, and a class or LBGTQ problem there. Many times that framework erases what happens to people who are subject to all of these things." AAPF team members "use art and other projects to show how people are experiencing intersectional harms, such as mothers of women killed by the police, or young girls expelled from school. We work directly with advocates and communities to develop ways they can better see these problems and better intervene in advocacy."[11]

Crenshaw's work is important for libraries to engage with and understand. She was a keynote speaker at IDEAL '19: Advancing Inclusion, Diversity, Equity, and Accessibility in Libraries and Archives, hosted by The Ohio State University Libraries. This conference aimed to foster awareness and appreciation of workplace diversity issues through the exploration of exemplary practice, contemporary theory, thought leadership, and strategy development for all those in the academic and public library, archives, and museum sectors. During the conference's opening session, Crenshaw challenged the group of more than 650 library colleagues from the United States and Canada to defend the legitimacy of inclusion and intersectionality. She discussed competing ideologies and how important it is to level the playing field for underserved populations.

Understanding your privilege and intersectionality will aid you in promoting the core principles of openness and learning. Such understanding will not only make you and your team more open to learning and hearing voices in a deeper way; you will be better equipped to help participants be more open to learning from people who may be different from them. The Madison Public Library (MPL) used an equity framework to design "Tell Us," a community conversation process. The library partnered with diverse agencies who in turn brought together racially diverse community members to discuss challenges they faced. Some of the partners were the Urban League, a YWCA shelter for families experiencing homelessness, and the community-based organization Unidos, among others. Importantly these conversations were not held at the library—they took place in homes, schools, and community spaces—and the community partners drove the topics.

By creating a model where agencies and individuals took ownership of the conversation, MPL was able to elicit information about the deeper values and aspirations of people who have not traditionally participated in library forums. This partnership-based model also enabled MPL to reach more people, including non-users, and ensured a level of racial diversity among respondents that matched or exceeded city demographics. Recommendations from these conversations informed the library's 2016 strategic plan and helped identify the need for new services on Madison's east side, where MPL is now building a new library.[12]

Moreover, understanding power and privilege is a step toward creating more inclusive planning processes, NCDD's core principle number one.

AN INTENTIONAL PRACTICE

We live in a society that still marginalizes people according to class, race, gender, place of birth, or any number of other facets of our identities. Until such time that we live in a truly egalitarian society, we need to be actively working toward making society more equitable.

The Government Alliance on Race and Equity (GARE) produced an issue brief on racial equity in public libraries. The brief noted, "While race-neutral approaches to library service may seem fair, colorblind or race-neutral practices often reproduce racial disparity, resulting in unfair access and outcomes. The fact that a person's race remains a principal determinant of health, safety, education and opportunity in the twenty-first century, should compel libraries to focus on race and its impact on our work."[13]

Put another way, it is not enough to simply be not racist; we must work to be anti-racist. Scholar Beverly Daniel Tatum uses the analogy of being on a moving walkway. The history and structures of racism are the walkway, and it is not enough to simply stop walking because you're still moving in a racist direction, just more slowly. It is also not enough to turn around; then you are still moving in a racist direction, just backward! In order to be anti-racist, you must actively walk in the opposite direction.[14] Simmons University Library has created an anti-oppression LibGuide (https://simmons.libguides.com/anti-oppression), which is a good place to start if you are at the beginning of your journey to more inclusive and authentic community engagement.

To create a culture of authentic and equitable community engagement within your organization, you'll have to engage in an ongoing intentional practice of actively working for inclusion and anti-oppression. It is important to make space for people to be themselves and find genuine connections to others.

This is not a passive activity or something that happens by happenstance on the organizational level, although when getting started, there is room for a range of participation styles on the individual employee level. GARE breaks this strategy into three broad action categories: Normalize (prioritizing equity), Organize (building internal capacity and partnering with others), and Operationalize (using equity tools and partnerships to inform your action plan). You can start by assessing your library on the following areas:

Normalize
- What steps could you take to increase a shared understanding of bias, racism, and racial equity?
- How does white cultural dominance impact people of color in your institution? What kind of culture shift is needed?
- How could you develop a clear racial equity vision?

Organize
- Who are the groups in your community working toward racial equity?
- How could you support community groups working to reduce disparities?
- How could you develop deep relationships with communities that have not been included in decision-making?

Operationalize
- What topics or decisions call for a Racial Equity Assessment?
- What action steps and measures will you take to achieve results?[15]

One key practice in creating equitable community engagement is to identify the individuals who would be most impacted by a policy or program and find ways to involve them in the decision process. This involvement could be achieved through facilitated large- or small-group conversations or even one-on-one conversations.

When working toward inclusion and equity in your community engagement programs, keep in mind that equity is not the same as equality. Treating everyone the same does not make a level playing field. The Center for Story-Based Strategy has designed an exercise to imagine a more equitable and inclusive future (figure 7.2). You may be familiar with the two images that illustrate the difference between equity and equality: three individuals of various heights are trying to watch a baseball game over a fence. Only one individual is tall enough to see over the fence. In the equality image, each person is given the same size box to stand on; however, the shortest person still cannot see over

FIGURE 7.2 | **THE FOURTH BOX SIMULATION GAME**

the fence. In the equity image, the tallest person doesn't get a box, the middle person gets one box, and the shortest person gets two. Now all three can see the game. A third image, labeled liberation, has no fence at all.[16]

In this example the fence is an unexamined assumption. However, there may be other unexamined assumptions, so the exercise offers a fourth box that is empty and asks people to imagine the story they would tell if there were no barriers and they were free to follow their dreams. Ellen Knutson has done this exercise with her students at the University of Illinois iSchool, and they have created a variety of different stories and had fruitful discussions about participating versus being a spectator and about issues of gender, race, physical abilities, and who gets left on the sidelines. This kind of creative thinking can lead to discussions of ways we can enact the equality, equity, and liberation we aspire to in our work. The Center for Story-Based Strategy offers free tools to facilitate this type of discussion with your team.

Sometimes when working toward greater inclusion in your community, the library does not have to be the main partner, yet can still be focused on the impact and action of the engagement process. As an example, the Beauregard

Parish Library in southwest Louisiana focused on inclusion by recognizing invisible or intangible barriers to participation. The senior adults in the community were not coming to technology classes at the library. Rather than dismissing the lack of attendance as a lack of interest, the library partnered with the Beauregard Council on Aging to create "All Hands on Tech," a program series that meets at the Council on Aging's space, which seniors were already regularly visiting.[17]

Honoring dates important to members of your community is also a way to frame engagement. June 28, 2019, marked the fiftieth anniversary of the police raid of the Stonewall Inn. The ensuing rebellion marked a turning point in LGBTQ+ liberation and is honored and celebrated through Pride Parades around the world. According to David Siders at The Public Library of Cincinnati and Hamilton County, "Pride is more than a parade. It's an opportunity to listen to, hire, and pay people in the LGBTQ+ community. It's a chance to volunteer with local grassroots organizations, speak up and support LGBTQ+ rights, and educate yourself and those around you. Pride shouldn't be something we celebrate and recognize just in June. These are all actions that can be taken year-round."[18] The Cincinnati Library hosted a series of events and exhibits to honor the milestones of Cincinnati Pride and Stonewall 50, including holding community conversations on coming out and transgender reality, creating a series of videos and podcasts that explore LGBTQ+ liberation, and facilitating a conversation about LGBTQ+ literature, media, and social media from the past to the present. Through projects and programs such as these, the library shows that it is a welcoming and safe space for the LGBTQ+ community and keeps an ongoing focus on inclusion and demographic diversity in its engagement work.

RELATIONSHIP BUILDING IS KEY

"You need to build the relationship before you need the relationship" is a mantra that our colleague Larry Payne at Houston Public Library often reminds us to focus on. The developers of the second edition of *Principles of Community Engagement* pointed out that "communities are not homogeneous entities; they are made up of diverse groups with different histories, social structures, value systems, and cultural understandings of the world."[19] Building strong relationships that are reciprocal and mutually beneficial will help you not only better understand your community but also develop deeper insights into how to equitably and authentically engage with even the most marginalized members of your community.

The focus on relationships helps move your engagement strategies from an informing stance to a more collaborative stance. Changing your paradigm to working *with* your community in all its diversity, rather than just providing services *for* your community, will have profound impacts on your library and how it builds inclusive programs that highlight the core principle of collaboration and shared purpose. For example, in Portland, Oregon, two librarians from Multnomah County Library, Amy Honisett and Kate Schwab, brought central library staff together with patrons experiencing homelessness for regular coffee and conversation sessions. These informal gatherings challenged the typical patterns of interaction, which often focused on behavior modification, and led to changes in how these two groups relate to each other. As the librarians worked with the patrons who were attending the coffee and conversation sessions, they made shifts in the program and even added programming, such as a writing program, for the group. The experiment garnered interest from management and librarians in other branches who also wanted to shift the way they relate to this group of patrons.[20] In an article in *Oregon Library Association Quarterly*, Honisett, Schwab, and Rachael Short noted, "Library staff who have practice talking to marginalized patrons will have more confidence helping a patron meet those information needs. Approaching the relationship in a way that demonstrates that we are not only providing a service but also meeting each other as individual people, makes the library more welcoming and allows us to provide relevant programming and services."[21]

Moreover, the shift to working *with* the community will aid in creating a more sustainable and participatory culture in your library. At the Topeka and Shawnee County Public Library in Topeka, Kansas, the team responsible for the library's new learn and play bus adapted the standard decision-making procedures to include fifteen-minute conversations with children's caregivers about their concerns. Earlier efforts to get community input focused on conversations with educational experts and other professionals and did not necessarily reveal what mattered most to the people who would use the learn and play bus. Including children and their caregivers in the discussions significantly changed how the bus is utilized. The goals now include children's social and emotional readiness for kindergarten instead of only academic success. The bus also provided the space for a caregivers' learning community to develop so that everyone's expertise and experiences could be shared. Additionally, staff training now includes active listening and how to become a learning facilitator rather than a teacher.[22] The relationships that form can lead to new ideas and new partnerships or programs that the librarians alone could not have developed on their own.

As libraries begin to focus on relationships and shift to working with the community, cultural competence is critical. Equity, diversity, and inclusion strategist DeEtta Jones reminds us that "cultural competence is more than an attitude; it is a skill set that requires investment and practice."[23] Becoming more culturally competent increases your ability to resolve conflict and can create

MOVING TOWARD ETHICAL AND INCLUSIVE THINKING IN AN ACADEMIC LIBRARY

In recent years, The Ohio State University (OSU) Libraries has undergone a transformation in how we approach our planning and services, with a shift toward the values of equity, diversity, and inclusion. In 2016 the faculty, staff, and administrators embarked upon a strategic planning process to clarify the organization's values and directions. This process involved an organizational assessment, gathering feedback from outside stakeholders (students, donors, faculty, staff, and administrators) and internal focus groups, and several rounds of feedback sessions for University Libraries faculty and staff.

University Libraries' final strategic plan includes the following Equity Value: "We advance diversity, inclusivity, access, and social justice." In addition, one of the plan's six strategic directions is "Engage for Broader Impact: pursue initiatives aligned with university priorities to promote a more engaged and better informed society." The two Focus Areas that help University Libraries in its engagement efforts are (a) underserved and at-risk communities and (b) campus and external partnerships.[1] It is with the equity value and the "Engage for Broader Impact" direction in mind that the organization has developed a culture of authentic and equitable community engagement.

Since the adoption of the new strategic plan, the Libraries has offered training for management and staff across the organization, covering topics such as "We're Diverse, Now What," "Active Bystander Training and How to Be an Ally," and "Identifying and Confronting Unconscious Bias in the Workplace," with additional sessions and topics scheduled in the future. During the planning of the IDEAL '19: Advancing Inclusion, Diversity, Equity, and Accessibility in Libraries and Archives, held at OSU in collaboration with the Association of Research Libraries and the Association of College and Research Libraries, the OSU organizers held active bystander training for all conference volunteers, many of whom would be working at the registration desk and in the session rooms where sensitive topics related to equity, diversity, and inclusion would be discussed. This training is also a part of University Libraries' commitment to authentic and equitable community engagement.

The strategic planning process was key to the success of OSU Libraries' engagement efforts. Because the entire organization was involved in defining its values and setting the strategic directions, it was understood and hoped (although voluntary) that faculty and staff would find a way to contribute to and support community engagement both on campus and throughout central Ohio. Since the strategic plan was adopted, nearly 100 of the Libraries' 240

full-time employees have been directly involved with an outreach or community engagement program. Librarians and staff serve as mentors for Big Brothers Big Sisters; others volunteer at the Mid-Ohio Foodbank. For the past three
summers, the Libraries have hosted high school students for paid internships
through which they gain real work experience, learn about academic libraries, and are exposed to the university through tours or guest speakers. Other
librarians and staff members have hosted programs focused on educating the
campus community about cultural diversity, cultural heritage, and significant
cultural events that have shaped our history.

NOTE
1. The Ohio State University Libraries, "Strategic Directions," https://library.osu.edu/
   strategic-directions.

more authentic and engaging experiences for groups that may be hesitant or
uncomfortable at your library and will help you focus on the core value of inclusion and demographic diversity. Many libraries across the country, including
The Ohio State University Libraries, have benefitted from training with Jones
and others who help facilitate these conversations that can feel difficult and
uncomfortable at times but are essential to the success of your organization
and community engagement.

AN ONGOING PROCESS

Building a culture of ethical and inclusive community engagement takes time
and patience. Start by listening to your stakeholders, which might include
students, faculty, staff, community members, community organizations, poli-
ticians, donors, trustees, and the like. Have discussions with them about their
perception of the library as a partner in the community and find out ways in
which they would like to engage with you. Begin building strategic partnerships
with individuals and organizations who share your values and goals. Host a
program that is sponsored by one of your partners, and provide volunteers to
assist, just to get your feet wet in community engagement. Think about joining forces with organizations that already have impactful programs that align
with your work. This approach will allow you to use the expertise, services,
or other resources that you currently have to make the program even better.
This association will also help staff and faculty feel more comfortable working

in this space, and the work will feel like an extension of what you do, rather than additional work.

There will be many challenges, but getting started and being open to learning and adjusting will be the keys to success. Listen, partner, execute, evaluate, iterate, and you will be well on your way to creating a culture of ethical and inclusive community engagement that is purposeful and impactful. Don't forget, we're all in this together!

NOTES

1. Margo Gustina and Eli Guinnee, "Why Social Justice in the Library? Outreach + Inreach," *Library Journal* (June 2017).

2. "IAP2 Spectrum of Public Participation," IAP2: International Association for Public Participation, 2018, https://cdn.ymaws.com/www.iap2.org/resource/resmgr/pillars/Spectrum_8.5x11_Print.pdf.

3. Working Together Project, *Community-Led Libraries Toolkit* (Vancouver, BC: Vancouver Public Library, 2008), 16. https://www.vpl.ca/sites/vpl/public/Community-Led-Libraries-Toolkit.pdf.

4. Tom Atlee, Stephen Buckley, John Godec, Reynolds-Anthony Harris, Sandy Heierbacher, Leanne Nurse, Steve Pyser and Stephanie Roy McCallum, *Core Principles for Public Engagement* (National Coalition for Dialogue and Deliberation, the International Association for Public Participation, and the Co-Intelligence Institute, 2009), 3, http://ncdd.org/rc/wp-content/uploads/2010/08/PEPfinal-expanded.pdf.

5. American Library Association, *Diversity Counts* (Chicago: American Library Association, 2007), www.ala.org/aboutala/offices/diversity/diversitycounts/divcounts. According to *Diversity Counts*, credentialed librarians are 88 percent white.

6. Peggy McIntosh, "White Privilege: Unpacking the Invisible Knapsack," ERIC (1988): 3–4.

7. John Berry, "White Privilege in Library Land," *Versed: Bulletin of the Office for Diversity, American Library Association* (June 2004): 1.

8. Nicole A. Cooke, *Information Services to Diverse Populations: Developing Culturally Competent Library Professionals* (Santa Barbara, CA: Libraries Unlimited, 2017), 3.

9. Multnomah County Library, *Equity and Inclusion 2018 Report*, https://multcolib.org/sites/default/files/MCL-2018-Equity-and-Inclusion-Report-JAN20.pdf.

10. Kimberlé Williams Crenshaw, "Mapping the Margins: Intersectionality, Identity Politics, and Violence against Women of Color," *Stanford Law Review* 43, no. 6 (July 1991): 1241–99.

11. Columbia Law School, "Kimberlé Crenshaw on Intersectionality, More Than Two Decades Later," June 8, 2017, https://www.law.columbia.edu/pt-br/news/2017/06/kimberle-crenshaw-intersectionality.

12. Amy Sonnie, *Advancing Racial Equity in Public Libraries: Case Studies from the Field* (Government Alliance on Race and Equity), 27, https://www.racialequityalliance.org/resources/advancing-racial-equity-in-public-libraries-case-studies-from-the-field/.

13. Sonnie, *Advancing Racial Equity*, 6.

14. Beverly Daniel Tatum, *Why Are All the Black Kids Sitting Together in the Cafeteria? And Other Conversations about Race* (New York, NY: Basic Books, 2017).

15. Sonnie, *Advancing Racial Equity*, 15.

16. "The 4th Box," Center for Story-Based Strategy, www.storybasedstrategy.org.

17. Celise Reech-Harper, "Intangible Barriers: One Approach for Senior Adult Services," *Intersections: A Blog on Diversity, Literacy, and Outreach*, June 6, 2019, www.ala.org/advocacy/diversity/odlos-blog/hands-on-tech.

18. David Siders, "More Than a Parade: Stonewall 50 and Cincinnati Pride," *The Public Library of Cincinnati and Hamilton County Blog*, June 13, 2019, https://blog.cincinnatilibrary.org/Blog/pride2019.

19. Clinical and Translational Science Awards (CTSA) Consortium's Community Engagement Key Function Committee, *Principles of Community Engagement*, 2nd ed., NIH Publication No. 11-7782 (Washington, DC: National Institutes of Health, 2011), 10, https://www.atsdr.cdc.gov/communityengagement/pdf/PCE_Report_508_FINAL.pdf.

20. Ellen Knutson, "Libraries and Community: From Informing to Engaging," *National Civic Review* 107, no. 3 (2018).

21. Amy Honisett, Rachael Short, and Kate Schwab, "Building Community at the Library with Coffee and Conversation," *Oregon Library Association Quarterly* (Winter 2017): 24.

22. Knutson, "Libraries and Community."

23. DeEtta Jones, "Essentials of Cultural Competence Course," https://courses.deettajones.com/courses/essentials-of-cultural-competence.

8

CULTURE SHIFT
The Path to
Becoming Community-Centered

ERICA FREUDENBERGER *and* SUSAN HILDRETH

L et's face it: change is hard. Although the brave among us enthusiastically embrace new opportunities, many find it uncomfortable or even traumatic. But if libraries are going to commit to being engaged organizations, anchoring their work in the aspirations of their communities, doing so requires both organizational and personal change.

By embracing community engagement, we shift our focus outward, to the people and socio-ecosystem we serve. Doing so requires recalibrating not only what we do but how we do it—including the daily staffing and running of our libraries. As we encourage and support change in our communities, we often face opposition when we attempt to implement it at our workplace. As the Building Movement Project points out,

> engaging in social change efforts may involve fundamental changes in the organization's values, strategy, and structure. It also may include working with staff in other organizations, advocating for policy changes, and engaging constituents in new ways that require difficult conversations about equality and power.[1]

Those difficult conversations, if effective, lead to more change—in programs, policies, priorities, and even job titles and duties. One of the challenges is letting go of old ideas about how we do things and relinquishing our power and control as we make space for community members to play an active role in decision-making. How does this happen? By making time to develop deep, authentic relationships across silos to build and leverage our capacity and to involve more voices in our decision-making. We have to be ready to relinquish our ideas about being neutral, noncontroversial spaces and commit wholeheartedly to the responsibility we have to foster the development of resilient, thriving communities. "Finally, we must let go of outdated ideas about neutrality when it comes to social justice principles. We must organize alongside our communities to support movements for social justice and human rights. . . . We occupy a key role in the sharing of stories and the building of a shared experience. We must take leadership to make our institutions embody the social justice values of dignity, human rights, community wellbeing, solidarity, equity, and belonging."[2]

How do we move beyond traditional services and create community-centered libraries? By examining our assumptions, making changes that may not benefit us directly but create value for our community by building social capital, and welcoming the public in authentic ways in which they can share in decision-making and implementation of services and can help lead equitably. We recognize that this shift is not a quick fix. To change the DNA of an organization requires centering the people in our community as equals in an ongoing, conscious assessment and decision-making process that benefits all. And it means letting go of things that make us comfortable.

This chapter will address the nuts and bolts of creating an engaged library, from navigating change to getting buy-in from staff, trustees, and friends. We'll explore how a community engagement lens creates a new way of understanding and providing library services, how to reorganize a library to align with community aspirations, and how to embrace dissent. Finally, we'll connect personal realignment with that of the institution and provide examples of organizations that are in the process of becoming engaged.

CHANGE MANAGEMENT

Creating a community-centered library requires a significant shift in theory and practice, including internal strategy about staffing, policies, and priorities. This shift doesn't happen overnight or by accident. It must be deliberate, be intentional, and have dedicated resources to be successful.

As Richard Kong, director of Skokie (Illinois) Public Library, which serves sixty-six thousand residents in a suburb of Chicago, explains, it can take years for meaningful change to take hold. Kong began in 2013 and admits, "It's still a work in progress. Our community partners are also getting used to partnering. We have to go out and model what we're trying to do."[3] The library's efforts have resulted in increased inclusion and equity, creating resilient families, partnering with local schools to focus on early literacy initiatives, and serving people with disabilities. But how do we begin to implement such a change?

REVISING JOB TITLES, DESCRIPTIONS, AND RESPONSIBILITIES

After taking part in the American Library Association's Libraries Transforming Communities (ALA LTC) cohort in 2014, Nancy Ledeboer, executive director of the Spokane County (Washington) Library District (SCLD), made changes in librarians' titles and job descriptions reflecting the commitment to community engagement. The new job description revamped the traditional role of the reference librarian. Librarians were now expected to get out from behind the desk and go into the community.

The new position of community librarian required buy-in from staff. Anything that previously was in the "this position may" category of the job description was now an essential part of the job. This adjustment made the changes feel less seismic and more incremental. Previous roles weren't eradicated; rather, organizational priorities were refined and redefined. Staff were able to work with the community precisely because of their experience in their previous duties.

By sharing tasks, all staff had time and opportunity to go into the community. "Librarians started attending city council meetings a few times a year. We went to school board meetings, arranged for programs outside the library, connected with chambers of commerce and higher education institutes. By leaving the library, we connected with people who didn't use our services," explained Aileen Luppert, the managing librarian of the Spokane County Library District's Spokane Valley Library branch.[4] Her presence at the Greater Valley Support Network, a coalition of stakeholders working with people experiencing homelessness, led to her being appointed to the leadership team and, eventually, chairing the initiative.

At Skokie Public Library, Kong began "a massive restructuring of our organizational chart" in fall 2013 with the former director, Carolyn Anthony. Embracing the idea of turning outward, Anthony and Kong rethought the role of adult and youth services staff and created a Community Engagement Department, which, Kong admits, "was a huge shift." Staff in the Community Engagement Department are expected to be outside the library more than in their offices. Rather than retaining the traditional titles of adult and youth services, Anthony and Kong created subject specialists who work with different populations in the community. "One [specialist] focuses on small businesses, attending meetings on economic development and provid[ing] training for small businesses and entrepreneurs," explained Kong. "Another focuses on serving immigrant[s] and refugees, and another on senior services."[5]

The library's early development and youth services position partners with young parents and child-care centers. The school services librarian focuses on working with school librarians, teachers, and administrators in both private and public schools. The library also has a robust bookmobile service, which provides programs as well as materials. The new positions are part of a strategy of "neighborhood services," defined by Kong as "trying to understand the needs of specific, small neighborhoods, rather than [designing] solutions for the larger community of sixty-six thousand."[6]

CREATING A TIME LINE FOR CHANGE

At SCLD, Ledeboer created a six-month time line and put Patrick Roewe, the deputy director (now executive director), in charge of implementing the change. Roewe used the metaphor of riding a bus to illustrate the impending changes, explaining that the organization was beginning a journey. He made it clear that in six months things would look different.

Roewe was enthusiastic, reassuring staff that there was room for everyone on the bus and encouraging everyone to get on the bus, but cautioning that the bus would be leaving. The following six months were spent training staff, answering questions, and acknowledging that everyone was going through a significant learning period, which required flexibility and adjustments. The change was successful because of the management team's focus on communicating why the changes were necessary so that staff could understand the reasoning behind the changes. Management also had to be able to articulate what would be different moving forward and to respond to staff questions and input throughout the process, creating an opportunity for buy-in. Because management openly acknowledged that ongoing adjustments might be necessary, staff understood the risks involved and were more comfortable trying new things, knowing that the administration would not penalize them if something failed. The creation of an environment in which failure is seen as a positive step forward in iterating change is critical to the success of any significant organizational shift.

Six years later, the changes—though not universally loved initially—are thoroughly ingrained. Some staff, reluctant to embrace the new vision of library service, opted to move on or retire. The staff who remained have settled into their new roles. The new staff assume that the role of community librarian is status quo and routinely spend time outside the library working with the community. "To them, community aspirations have always been the driving force for why we do what we do in the way we do it," says Luppert.[7]

It is essential to recognize that the changes made at SCLD were relatively easy to make quickly because SCLD's workforce is not unionized. In a unionized environment, it may take more than six months to accomplish a similar shift and require extensive discussions, yet this critical culture shift is vital.

COMMUNITY ENGAGEMENT IN A UNION ENVIRONMENT

At the Springfield (Massachusetts) City Library, staff working in eight branches and the central library have a choice of two unions for representation. The library serves a diverse community of 154,000, with a large and growing Latinx population. As one of the libraries that took part in the ALA LTC cohort, the Springfield City Library embraced community engagement. Due to its unions, the library didn't have the latitude that SCLD had in changing job descriptions. Instead, Jean Canosa Albano, the assistant director for public services, has revamped job titles and descriptions as positions have become vacant. The new job descriptions use more inclusive language and have a broader range of duties than the previous positions.

The most significant change, says Canosa Albano, is in recruitment—how the library markets open positions and the questions job candidates are asked. During the screening, a candidate is asked, "Why Springfield?," says Canosa Albano. "This gives us a sense of whether they have a feel of what the community is like and to find out what is attracting them to work and live here. Do they have the mindset of being a community-centered library?"[8] Other interview questions include the following:

- What do you consider the three most important roles for today's librarian?
- How does a librarian respond to needs in the Springfield community?
- What does community engagement look like or mean to you in a public library?
- How do you ensure responsiveness to community needs and changes?

The other change in hiring is "what we're listening for," says Canosa Albano. "I don't want to hear that people are good at searching the web, but that they're interested in doing community-centered programming. We're listening for people who are going to be great listeners and are excited about getting involved in community engagement."[9]

Canosa Albano's approach is mirrored in the Sacramento (California) Public Library and the Seattle (Washington) Public Library, both of which are unionized. Although the focus on community engagement has not resulted in significant changes in job descriptions in either institution, what has changed are the job advertisements, which focus on applicants' commitment to equitable service. Interview questions have also changed to include awareness of diversity, inclusion, and community engagement.

Libraries working with unions should consider including a union representative in developing plans for service and job description changes to provide for a better understanding of and buy-in to the value and necessity of the changes.

CULTURE SHIFT

To paraphrase Albert Einstein, it is folly to imagine that we will get different results without changing our actions. If we want to create a community-led, engaged library, we cannot rely on the skills and services that work in traditional libraries. Library policies and procedures must incorporate community input; staff expertise in empathy, interpersonal competence, and open-mindedness is essential.

At Skokie Public Library, shifting the culture meant a lot of conversation—with individuals, groups, and teams. "It was important to reinforce what we're doing, why we're doing it, and acknowledging the difficulties of change and respecting it," says Kong. "We understand that people will go through emotional stuff with change." Acknowledging the importance of culture, the library created an internal culture statement (see the accompanying sidebar) separate from its strategic plan that discusses "who we want to be for each other."[10]

"We put our organizational culture statement on every job description and tell all applicants to read it and apply only if the statement resonates with them," says Kong. "People, especially millennials, want to work for mission-driven and value-driven organizations."[11] Since creating the internal culture statement, the library has seen internal satisfaction improve from 50 to 80 percent.

Valerie Wonder, community engagement manager at the Seattle Public Library, describes the shift in perspective this way: "Whereas five years ago the common approach was 'I love knitting so I should host a knitting program,' now any time a new program idea comes up the first question from staff is, 'Did this idea come from the community?'"[12]

After the Sacramento Public Library engaged the special needs community, it began to hire staff with special needs, reported Kathy Middleton, the library's deputy director.[13] This shift means patrons with special needs are represented not as separate from the library but as an integral part of the organization. As Sandra Singh writes, "People want to see themselves represented in the library and to have an opportunity to participate."[14] When we invite people into our

SKOKIE PUBLIC LIBRARY CULTURE STATEMENT
We are Skokie Public Library.

We serve the community, and we *are* a community.

Each of us is a whole person with individual experiences and a unique perspective. Our diversity is our strength, and we treat one another the same way we treat our patrons, starting with a belief that others' intentions are good. As colleagues, we respect, value, support, and encourage one another. We have the courage to collaborate because we recognize that we are better together, and we are committed to direct, open-minded communication.

We share a passion for learning and partnering with others to build a better community. All of us are generous with our time, talent, and resources. Whether contributing to innovations, or continuing established practices, we stay flexible, mindful, and dedicated. We support thoughtful experimentation, and we gain insight from what we do and share that with each other, even when it doesn't work out the way we'd hoped. We pause to celebrate our successes, and we leave room to experience joy in our work and our colleagues, because together we form a vibrant whole organization.

libraries, our organizations become stronger and more resilient because of the diversity of abilities, talents, and expertise.

BUILDING CAPACITY THROUGH PROFESSIONAL DEVELOPMENT

The Kitsap Regional Library in Washington State restructured its Public Services Department to create a community engagement manager position, currently held by Lisa Lechuga. Her role is to "foster community engagement activities and co-creative program design."[15] In addition to creating a new position, the library is working on developing new skills to support its focus. Staff receive training related to the public participation spectrum, facilitation, design thinking, equity, and trauma-informed service. Although the library's efforts in community engagement are relatively new, Lechuga points to the success of the 2017 levy ballot measure as indicative of the success of the library's work with community partners to inform library services. The work, according to Lechuga, has helped the library develop "stronger relationships and ties to community partners." The next step is "to develop measures so that we can better report on the impact, and we need to build capacity to analyze and report back on the input received from the community."[16]

Skokie Public Library sent everyone in the Community Engagement Department to community engagement training and has now expanded the initiative to include additional staff from other departments as well. Doing so has provided a common language and approach to their work, which reinforces the library's culture shift.

"Early on, the community engagement team developed a mantra—'We listen. We learn. We connect. We create responsive solutions to Skokie's needs,'" says Lorrie Hansen, a community engagement librarian for K–8 school services.[17] The library's commitment to community engagement has resulted in hosting community conversations, embedding the library into the community, and developing new services for the community.

The library uses community conversations "to include voices of people who have traditionally been marginalized because of their abilities, mental health, language and status as newcomers to the country, race, and income," says Hansen. The information collected has influenced the library's strategic planning process, and, like the Spokane County Library District, the library prioritized staff participation in community committees. Library staff are essential contributors to these conversations and expand their listening and collaboration skills as a result of their involvement. "Beyond listening, we actively contribute to the discussions and support projects and events as committee members, from writing grants to helping plan and implement events."[18]

COLLABORATIVE PARTNERSHIPS

As Skokie Public Library develops new programs and services, it has encouraged the community to step forward and play a role in the library through volunteerism. Volunteers take part in literacy programs and are encouraged to take action in other community agencies. "In collaboration with the local high school district and nonprofit partners, students and young adults with disabilities deliver library materials to homebound patrons, creating a win-win opportunity and unique twist on a traditional service," writes Hansen, who points out that "volunteers are both strengthening and creating community."[19]

By nurturing collaborative partnerships with other community stakeholders, Skokie Public Library has been able to create new collaborative structures focused on community aspirations and issues. "Three collective impact initiatives have formed around creating a more welcoming and equitable community; a positive environment for healthy early childhood development; and a resilient community in response to the negative effects of adverse childhood experiences," writes Hansen. "The library has played various roles in these ongoing efforts, including convenor, facilitator, project coordinator, host, and active supporter."[20]

Five years in, the library's commitment to community engagement is influencing how organizations collaborate in Skokie. "The library is connecting individuals and organizations to resources, opportunities, and each other," writes Hansen. "Together with our partners, we are learning to work in new ways to have a longer-term, greater community impact."[21]

MAKING COMMUNITY ENGAGEMENT A REALITY, ONE STEP AT A TIME

The Seattle Public Library is committed to actively engaging with and providing service to underserved communities as well as furthering racial equity and social justice in the library and the community. To realize these lofty goals, the library has developed an efficient and effective program focused on outreach, programming, and engagement. The library commits annually to working on three to four projects with small nonprofits serving under-resourced neighborhoods for about six months. For each project, small cohorts of library staff work closely with colleagues from the nonprofits on specific service initiatives. The nonprofits are given $3,000 per project to provide support for the initiative. There is an investment of staff time on the part of the library and the partner organization. This in-depth yet focused community engagement provides opportunities for accountability for the library and the partner organization.

These projects also provide an intensive space for staff to work closely together. The effort serves as a leadership development opportunity for the library staff. It is particularly beneficial for staff of color who may not have the opportunity to undertake special projects in their regular job assignments. These small investments in underserved communities make a big difference—in those neighborhoods and for the library staff.

ENGAGING KEY STAKEHOLDERS

Support from and endorsement by the library's governing body are critical to success. When Erica Freudenberger returned from the first meeting of the ALA LTC cohort, she held an Aspirations Exercise, developed by the Harwood Institute for Public Innovation, with her board. The exercise asks participants to consider aspirations and find common ground for working with others:

Take a moment to focus on your community aspirations and to identify next steps you want in creating change. Add your aspirations, challenges, and the new conditions to create in the spaces provided below.

- **Aspirations:** My aspirations for my community are: _____
- **Challenges:** The challenges we face in reaching these aspirations are: _____

- **New conditions:** The changes needed in my community to reach our aspirations are: _____[22]

The exercise provided an opportunity for the board to experience the work the library would be doing in the community. The process allowed the board to see the value in shifting the conversation from asking what people wanted from the library to asking the community what vision it had for itself.

By bringing in the board early, Freudenberger was able to show how and why she would be spending time outside the library, collecting information about the community. The board committed to the process and worked with Freudenberger to identify groups and individuals who should be involved in the information-gathering stage—either as volunteers to collect the information or as participants in the conversations.

In implementing significant changes in service philosophy, the library must consider the local political landscape. Librarians must understand the points of power or levers of change in their library and in their community. Engagement by and support from the library's governing body or organization, an administrative or advisory board, and a city or county manager or elected council are critical. Libraries should consider partnering with a city manager, a mayor, or other appointed or elected officials to help lead the community engagement initiative. By remaining open to the input of others, and making space for community and nonprofit leaders, libraries can build capacity to create ownership of and support for the process and implementation of change.

One challenge of community engagement is that library boards and staff often do not reflect the diversity of the communities they serve. It is the responsibility of library leadership and appointing authorities to ensure that the composition of the library board reflects the diversity of the community. As boards become more diverse, the voices and priorities of the community are more effectively represented. Engaging a variety of community members in the library planning process will result in a more authentic reflection of the community, which leads to serving the community more effectively.

Library Friends and Foundation groups are also critical organizations to engage in this service shift. In some cases, they represent more traditional or mainstream segments of the community. They may provide significant support to the library and could be influential advocates in engaging the community as well as providing access to valuable community networks. Including these vital support groups in the conversation about community-driven services is an effort that must occur and, it is hoped, will provide an important voice of support.

ENGAGED LEADERSHIP

Often, when we think of leadership, we have an image of a charismatic person who has accumulated experience and wisdom with a vision of where an organization or community should head. Engaged leadership moves away from the model of one or two specific leaders and instead embraces the idea that any community has many leaders. This distributed leadership model acknowledges the variety of expertise, talent, and ability that exists and recognizes that people lead as their specific skills are needed. To effectively catalyze change, engaged leaders recognize that initiative can come from anywhere and should be willing to embrace and promote leadership wherever it arises.

David Mathews, the president and CEO of the Kettering Foundation, in a study of communities grappling with serious challenges, wrote, "What stood out in the higher-achieving community was not so much the characteristics of the leaders as their number, their location, and, most of all, the way they interacted with other citizens. The higher-achieving community had ten times more people providing initiative than communities of comparable size. . . . And its leaders functioned not as gatekeepers but as door openers, bent on widening participation."[23]

In recognizing and inviting others to lead, engaged leaders must be willing to let go of the idea of being an expert and embrace the concepts of learning alongside our communities and of working with, not for, the people we serve. Doing so also means inviting people into the library, not only to use our services but also to take an active role in planning services, leading programs, and setting priorities. Engaged leadership acknowledges the power of social capital, demands that librarians be both authentic and vulnerable to the communities we serve as we fearlessly learn with others, and understands that reciprocity and trust lead to voluntary cooperation.

There's no safety net in engaged leadership. It requires a recalibration of our thinking and establishes new, community-centered priorities. It also demands support from the administration and governing body and allows for the prototyping and iteration of ideas—not all of which will be successful. When initiatives are not successful, it's essential to assess what went wrong and learn from it, but not to allow a failure to stymie future efforts and growth.

ENGAGED STAFF

Librarians can lead from any level, but in some settings radical, nontraditional change may be more readily adopted by leaders in the organization than by rank-and-file staff. To help staff ease into their new roles, Canosa Albano used the Harwood Institute's Ask Exercise with the staff at the Mason Square Branch Library, where the library system's community engagement work was based. The Ask Exercise states,

> We want to get a sense of people's aspirations for their community and learn about the kind of community they want to create. Introduce yourself and say, "We're trying to learn more about people's aspirations for their community. Would you be willing to answer four quick questions?"
> - What kind of community do you want to live in?
> - Why is that important to you?
> - How is that different from how you see things now?
> - What are some of the things that need to happen to create that kind of change?[24]

By working through the exercise, the staff had a chance to understand the practice and think about their role in a new way. "For the most part, people reacted well, but there were some who were less excited," says Canosa Albano. "Going forward, we hired people who are more favorably disposed to community engagement as others left or retired."[25]

In addition to training staff, Canosa Albano incorporated community engagement into the library's practices, including the language used in monthly reports. Instead of collecting quantitative data about how many programs were held and the number of attendees, she collects narrative highlights that demonstrate the impact a department is having on the community through programming, services, outreach, or partnerships. "If you know you have to report on something, you have to pay attention to it," says Canosa Albano. Staff now submit requests for purchases that will enhance services for the public instead of budget requests. Staff also report back on aspirations, concerns, and other things they hear from the community, even if it isn't related to the library. "You can't make everyone come around, but you can show how it benefits us and hope that they will begin to reconsider how we're moving forward," says Canosa Albano.[26]

Inviting in community expertise may empower the community yet threaten the staff. Library staff expertise is valuable and integral to the success of library services, and it is essential to value and delineate the unique skills provided by staff. In community-centered libraries, the community is setting the priorities for services, programming, and collections. Once priorities are established, the role of librarians and their expertise in providing those services are critical. The community can identify topics for adult programming—and librarians, with community input, can assemble the resources and activities that make that programming a success!

For staff to be engaged and thriving in a library moving from traditional to more community-based values, library leadership must establish a culture of acceptance of fast failure, an environment in which prudent risk-taking is a value. Managers must support new service approaches and encourage staff to take on unique initiatives. By doing so, the capacity of staff to embrace change and authentic services is boundless.

NOT ALWAYS AN EASY PATH

The commitment to authentic community-centered libraries is not an easy one; it can challenge the traditional view of libraries as neutral or noncontroversial spaces by focusing instead on convening the community and helping residents take agency to address a wide range of issues. But taking on those issues is key for the twenty-first-century library.

For Richard Kong, this approach has "transformed the way we attack any of our work. The effort to connect with, listen to, and partner with our community is ingrained in what we do. It's not something that we have to remind ourselves about constantly; it's our starting place."[27]

During this transformational journey, conflict may occur with local officials, patrons, board members, and staff. Turf issues often arise, and confusion about the library's role may occur. By investing time to build trusted relationships, you may find it easier to address many of those issues. Leaders must be willing to deal with conflict respectfully and responsibly. Change may need to be incremental and not necessarily supported by all parties. Often having one to two committed, strategic individuals can clear the path for the future without having to wait for consensus by all.

The benefits of partnerships often outweigh any difficulties. "It's so much more rewarding to work together on projects and not feel like the library is going to swoop in and solve everyone's issues, but we'll be at the center of whatever the community feels is important and wants to do," says Kong.[28] There also will be many new and meaningful relationships with segments of the community that the library has never served. At the Springfield City Library, the number of partnerships has grown exponentially. "We are involved in weekly meetings with state police, local police, city government, community residents, and representatives from stakeholder groups—all of whom want to work together to create a safer, livable community," says Canosa Albano. These relationships have led to collective programming and planning, with the library now involved in more than five thousand programs each year. Although the path has not always been smooth, Canosa Albano is a champion of the process. "It's too easy for us to get into our bubbles," she said. "If we're not paying attention to our communities, what are we even doing here?"[29]

Libraries will fulfill their true missions when they respect and support their communities in achieving their vision. By embracing community engagement, libraries have the opportunity to model the type of behavior and relationships we value, overcoming systemic and cultural barriers to create organizations that reflect and celebrate the communities we serve. It takes the thoughtful dedication of library leadership to inspire supporters and staff to retool libraries to achieve these goals. Although it may be challenging to let go of our assumptions and see failure as an opportunity to grow, libraries must embrace the challenge to become the valuable civic institutions we want to see in the world.

NOTES

1. Building Movement Project, *Nonprofits Integrating Community Engagement Guide* (2015), 2.
2. Sarah Lawton, "Reflections on Gender Oppression and Libraries," *Public Libraries Online* (March 5, 2018), http://publiclibrariesonline.org/2018/03/reflections-on-gender-oppression-and-libraries/.
3. Richard Kong, telephone interview by Erica Freudenberger, August 14, 2019.
4. Aileen Luppert, e-mail message to author, July 13, 2019.
5. Kong, interview.
6. Kong, interview.
7. Luppert, e-mail message.
8. Jean Canosa Albano, telephone interview by Erica Freudenberger, August 26, 2019.
9. Canosa Albano, interview.
10. Kong, interview.
11. Kong, interview.
12. Valerie Wonder, telephone interview by Susan Hildreth, August 6, 2019.
13. Kathy Middleton, telephone interview by Susan Hildreth, August 1, 2019.
14. Sandra Singh, "Introduction," *Community-Led Libraries Toolkit* (Vancouver, BC: Vancouver Public Library, 2008), 8.
15. Lisa Lechuga, e-mail message to author, July 7, 2019.
16. Lechuga, e-mail message.
17. Lorrie Hansen, e-mail message to author, July 7, 2019.
18. Hansen, e-mail message.

19. Hansen, e-mail message.

20. Hansen, e-mail message.

21. Hansen, e-mail message.

22. Harwood Institute, "Aspirations," Libraries Transforming Communities, www.ala.org/tools/sites/ala.org.tools/files/content/LTC_Aspirations_0.pdf.

23. David Mathews, *Leaders or Leaderfulness? Lessons from High-Achieving Communities* (Dayton, OH: Kettering Foundation, 2016), 2.

24. Harwood Institute, "Ask," Libraries Transforming Communities, www.ala.org/tools/sites/ala.org.tools/files/content/Ask%20Exercise.pdf.

25. Canosa Albano, interview.

26. Canosa Albano, interview.

27. Kong, interview.

28. Kong, interview.

29. Canosa Albano, interview.

9

EMPOWERING VOLUNTEERS TO BUILD COMMUNITY

NANCY KIM PHILLIPS

W ho does community engagement at your library? Regardless of the staff who are given community engagement responsibilities, chances are that there is not enough time to pursue all the opportunities that arise when a library extends its gaze outward to the community. At Skokie Public Library, volunteers offer their time, abilities, and passions to expand the library's community engagement capacity from twelve staff members, including a part-time volunteer specialist, to an additional 130 people in the most recent year.

Whether for a one-time event or an ongoing activity, volunteers of all ages and abilities work behind the scenes and provide direct service, offering unique perspectives and skills that build the library's knowledge and understanding. Through community conversations, we learned that people yearn for meaningful connections. Volunteers forge bonds as they interact with others, an important aspect of creating community. The following examples highlight ways in which volunteers participate in community engagement at Skokie Public Library by delivering services and programs driven by an identified community need or desire, often in collaboration with partner organizations.

READ TO ME: PROMOTING EARLY LITERACY WHILE BUILDING STRONGER PARTNERSHIP

Early literacy and storytime are often the bread and butter of youth services at public libraries. Skokie Public Library has a long history of taking storytime out to home day-care providers, child-care centers, and preschools. When the library shifted its community approach to listen more, we asked early childhood providers how we might support them, their children, and families.

SCC Early Childhood Centers (SCC), a local, privately owned provider that has since become Skokie's only Head Start/Early Head Start site, responded. Although SCC values group storytime, their vision was for every child to have the experience of being read to individually, knowing that not all its families practiced this at home. However, this goal was not feasible for SCC's staff to accomplish on their own. SCC and the library, with volunteer help, identified a shared goal of supporting Skokie's community aspiration that its children be ready for kindergarten.

SCC and the library launched the Read to Me program in 2015, with the library recruiting, training, and supporting volunteers who share books and songs individually with children in SCC classrooms. To the delight of all involved, the program has expanded over time, with fifteen volunteers covering approximately 175 children ages 0 to 5 at three locations weekly, requiring ongoing coordination between partners. The children enjoy sharing books and songs within the context of warm and trusting relationships. Teachers learn new rhymes and techniques to engage children. Fifty-four percent of parents and guardians report that the Read to Me parent engagement materials positively influenced interactions with their children at home. Building upon the strong Read to Me partnership, SCC's executive director has become active in the formation of an Early Childhood Alliance and other community-wide efforts that support healthy child development.

FROM CLASSROOM TO CONVERSATION: VOLUNTEERS EXPAND ENGLISH AS A SECOND LANGUAGE SERVICES

For more than twenty years, Skokie Public Library has hosted English for Speakers of Other Languages (ESOL) and citizenship classes taught by the local community college. In a community in which more than 40 percent of residents were born outside the United States and more than seventy languages are spoken at home, these are important programs. Yet the basics gained in a classroom setting are not sufficient to give some English learners enough confidence to use their new skills in public, and they do not know anyone with whom they can practice.

Through the library's ESL One-on-One tutoring program, volunteers meet weekly with individual learners to help address specific needs. For instance, an adult student can prepare for upcoming conferences with a child's teacher or tackle bewildering language challenges related to their jobs. A community engagement librarian interviews both prospective students and volunteers, makes the matches, reserves space for partners, and stays in regular touch with both sides to troubleshoot issues that may arise and make sure that individual goals are being met.

Although the library provides oversight and administrative support, volunteers are given freedom to tailor sessions to encourage conversation. Students often wonder why a volunteer would help a stranger learn English for free. Through ESL One-on-One, students not only practice English language skills but also gain awareness of the tradition of volunteerism in the United States. At the same time, volunteers gain respect for their students and a greater awareness of other cultures, which enhances their abilities to create a welcoming community environment. As one volunteer said, "I have become a link between them and the library's resources as well as developing a friendship that extends beyond our one hour a week meeting at the library."

ACTION BOOK CLUB: ENCOURAGING THE NEXT GENERATION OF COMMUNITY VOLUNTEERS

With a population of sixty-six thousand, Skokie has five public elementary school districts feeding into one high school district. Before reaching high school, students have few opportunities to meet peers from other districts or share an experience across all five districts. From conversations with parents and schools throughout the community, we also know that middle school students want to volunteer in the community but have limited options. In partnership with Skokie schools and the Community Animal Rescue Effort (C.A.R.E.) Adoption Center, Skokie Public Library facilitated an Action Book Club in which sixth graders read and discussed a book, met students from other schools in the community, and completed a service project.

Librarians selected a novel featuring a main character in middle school who volunteers at a no-kill animal shelter. They collaborated with the local C.A.R.E. facility to develop a community service project and identified school liaisons to recruit participants and schedule book discussions. The library team visited each school during student lunchtimes for book discussions, which were fun and social. Seventy-eight Action Book Club members held rich conversations, respecting each other's thoughts and opinions, even those different from their own. Finally, thirty-one students gathered in several groups at C.A.R.E., where they took turns reading to the animals. This activity allowed C.A.R.E to provide educational and advocacy outreach to teens and families in Skokie, one of the center's primary goals. One student reflected, "We all have different lives but are part of one big community family. Helping adds to the community and makes it more like a family." It is hoped that Action Book Club will have enduring effects in the way students view their roles as contributors to society.

VOCATIONAL VOLUNTEERS: GAINING SKILLS AND CONNECTIONS, CREATING A WIN-WIN-WIN

In addition to recruiting volunteers for the community engagement initiatives just described, Skokie Public Library's part-time volunteer specialist supports departments across the organization. Yet this responsibility is just half the job. Developing partnerships with organizations that work with people who have disabilities makes up the other half. It is magic when the two parts of this one position come together in creative and powerful ways.

When the library's volunteer/accessibility specialist began meeting with representatives from nonprofit organizations and the local high school, participants shared the ways in which people with disabilities struggle to find work. They need experiences in a workplace setting to develop skills that can be transferred to a job. In response, Skokie Public Library created a program through which people with disabilities volunteer at the library. Vocational volunteers have become indispensable, assisting with tasks such as refilling scratch paper and sharpening pencils at the catalog stations, washing toys from Youth Services, pulling books to be weeded from the collection, and much more. Accompanied by their coaches, volunteer teams from three organizations deliver books to homebound seniors, who welcome their arrival. Considering the delivery was once handled by library staff, it is a win for all.

Altogether, the volunteer/accessibility specialist has identified twenty-five jobs for vocational volunteers across the library, breaking down those jobs into easy-to-follow steps captured in pictures. The number of jobs continues to grow. Volunteers also practice punching a timeclock and having lunch in the staff room. In the past two years, the library is aware of nine former volunteers with disabilities who have secured paid employment, including several at the library. Also satisfying are smaller wins, such as a vocational volunteer who was assembling summer reading packages asking how he could win prizes too and getting excited about registering for the program. Library staff and patrons alike are enriched by having the opportunity to recognize people for their abilities rather than their limitations.

GETTING STARTED

Volunteers have played an integral role in community engagement at Skokie Public Library, increasing capacity, enriching the work, and developing bonds that create community. As indicated earlier in this chapter, there can be lots of moving parts in managing community engagement volunteers, especially within the context of a collaborative partnership. The process can take time, patience, ongoing communication, organization, project management, and relationship management skills.

However, it doesn't have to be complicated to begin integrating volunteers into community engagement. Start where you are, perhaps getting help with your existing behind-the-scenes work, before developing something new. Build on what you do well, and work with partners who know you. Listen to what the community wants and needs; those aspirations will likely resonate with potential volunteers too. Importantly, be open to what volunteers can do and who they might be. Both your library and community will benefit from their passion, creativity, and unique abilities.

CIVIL RIGHTS CENTER
Community Engagement and Special Collections

TASNEEM A. GRACE *and* ANDREA BLACKMAN

A group contacts our Special Collections Division. They have heard about the Civil Rights Center, about the photographs of the sit-ins, about the books and films that detail civil disobedience. They want to visit, but they want more than a typical sixty-minute historic tour.

They have heard that we also guide group discussions about bias, invisibility, and personal responsibility. They want to go deep.

So deep is where we take them, past the images of "Keep White Schools White" picket signs and grimacing protesters. Past lyrics of "We Shall Overcome" and "Swing Low, Sweet Chariot." Past big names like Dr. Martin Luther King Jr. and John Lewis.

Instead, these engagements are led by contemporary events, community-led questions, and collective response.

They come hungry, famished from the quiet surrounding names like Sandra Bland, Trayvon Martin, and Michael Brown. They come ready to contextualize their experiences, and we welcome them as witnesses to the cycle of struggle.

"What looks familiar?" we ask our guests.

"Everything," they tell us.

An image from 1960 of a Black man being yanked from a lunch counter by a white man reminds one patron of an assault that took place in Antioch, Tennessee, in 2019 in which a white man shot and killed several people of color in a Waffle House.

Another picture, also from 1960, of four thousand students marching in silent protest of a bombing reminds another student of Black Lives Matter marches, marches for children, for women's and immigrants' equality.

The potency of these reflections deepens the engagement and creates community through conversation and deliberate—not passive—engagement. Together we practice how to amiably disagree, how to inhale and share deep truths and risk the sting of saying too much in exchange for the shame of saying too little.

THE POWER OF NARRATIVES

Although we love libraries with a deep, unwavering passion, we are not trained librarians. As the associate director of community engagement and director of the Special Collections Division of the Nashville Public Library, we are a pair of educators, writers, and humanities scholars. Deep down we are also performance artists and poets. We relish the opportunity to share the stories of Nashville's prominent role in the civil rights movement with the pacing and purpose of storytellers.

But these are our personal attributes that we bring to the office; they are not what is required to thrive here.

Special Collections is an area of librarianship praised for its adoration, and protection, of the past. Often guests will visit us looking for "anything really, really old."

They want to see well-preserved scrapbooks, ship manifests, seventy-year-old high school annuals, yellowed newspaper clippings, military memoirs, census data, and slave records. For years, offering looks into antiquity was what made our collections "special."

In 2015 the way we shared historical narratives evolved from retrospective presentations to modern meditations on the distressing loop of historical events, especially those featuring social injustice, racism, and subjugation. Beginning with a request from our local police chief to introduce all Metro Nashville Police recruits to Nashville's history of social injustice, our presentations have become conversations.

Fortified by a belief in transparent communication, we use the art and science of listening and speaking to explore the human desire for connection and curiosity.

Our pulse quickens when we imagine the ways in which contemporary social issues mirror history. We visualize meandering yet defined roads that connect our stories of liberation, struggle, and transformation. Our greatest joy as library professionals is to usher our guests toward perspective shifts and personal activism.

We build bridges with words, conversation, and courage. Calling ourselves "question collectors," we use inquiry the way some use information: to rattle sensibilities and urge fresh understanding.

Although many people visit libraries for recreation and resources, we design deliberate engagement to encourage patrons and guests to move beyond curiosity toward introspection. Here, lead staff skilled in facilitation and program design invite conversations about sensitive subjects with the intention of examining social change and solidarity despite discomfort.

Few people call this process "fun." "Important" is often mentioned in survey feedback, but rarely joy. And yet we believe that tension and toil can ease us toward the fresh perspectives, courage, and honesty that define our engagements.

Because libraries are gathering spaces for information, we also work to create gatherings for deliberate dialogue.

Archival history roots the exchange. Then we pierce collective complacency with personal stories about the tough stuff: racism, social justice, bias, oppression, and revolution.

Society often juxtaposes the terms *myth* and *history* such that the former means "erroneous" and "untrue" whereas the latter implies "factual." We propose that *myth* and *history* can be two sides of the same coin. Both are stories we tell to explain the way things are or how we think things are supposed to be. Insofar as myths canonize our values, Plato called them "sublime lies."

Aristotle went a little farther, suggesting that such stories provide cultural cohesion (i.e., narratives we use to hold together a population divided by race, class, age, and gender). In this way, both myths and history convey a society's highest ideals and aspirations . . . even when evidence proves that we fall far short.

With designed engagement, myths and history can be dangerous delusions because they can be fictions propagated by principalities and powers to seduce and delude the population into compliance. And although our collections contain enough primary sources to make a history lover gasp, it is stories steeped in vulnerability and lived experiences that build bridges of connection and community.

DELIBERATE ENGAGEMENT

Our impact reflects our intention to host, join, and direct conversations about our collective identities, rather than create them.

Deliberate engagement is best understood as the practice of purposeful subjective interactions with our patrons. Rather than passively offering resources about various topics, we invent strategies for critical thought, analysis, and investigation. Our goal is to create experiences that nudge our patrons toward valuing differing narratives, contradictory "facts," and varied storytelling.

Here, our work seeks to groom marginalized communities for opportunities that require original thought, skillful debate, and bold sharing. Our engagements encourage community conversations as a passport to the type of cultural exploration that confronts stereotypes, challenges biases, and incites self-examination.

UNITED WE RISE AND FALL

Together we ask, "How do we as humankind create the world we live in today?" Always a jolting question, this opener reveals our level of collective complicity in how we experience the world. Consequently, we model the spirit of joined humanity by sharing our own contribution—gains and losses that arise from social ills. The Civil Rights Center, for example, exists to share the stories of survival and patience. It also exists because of the global legacy of injustice. We resist our pain, and we embrace it.

Illuminating such truths over the past five years has brought more than ten thousand people to our engagements with requests to explore racialized disconnect and confusion. Typically, we begin in the Civil Rights Center where everyone sits around a circular replica of a lunch counter, similar to those occupied by protesters during the 1950s and '60s. With the rhythm of a dance, our introductions and ice-breaking banter slide between us before we initiate each group with a simple question: "Why are you here?"

While one of us asks each guest to talk about what understanding the individual came with and what new ones the person hopes to gain, the other jots down what is shared:

- I hope to learn more about this city I live in.
- I want to understand why we are still talking about race.
- I want to learn what to say to my family when they say racist things.
- I want to know what it takes to be a real ally.

These responses guide the discussion by highlighting, and personalizing, the focus of the engagement; they do not, however, define the goal of our engagement. We remain committed to the hope that our participants leave the library with an evolved perspective on racism and personal accountability. A formula that constantly blends historical narratives with present-day dramas keeps us on task.

BUILDING A BROAD TABLE

The impact of discussion and hearing new stories is evident in the development of a community of human connection. As our community and country become increasingly divided, it is important to have places where people can gather and attempt to understand differing perspectives. The most effective way to address the divisiveness in our communities is to foster compassion that sparks from a desire to speak, listen, ask, and learn.

Creating space to amplify voices of people from the margins and the mainstream is a pathway toward community kinship. The focus should be on designing opportunities for preexisting communities to gather in libraries, rather than on assuming the role of giving voice to marginalized groups.

Deliberate engagement seeks to widen the table to make room for diverse influencers, rather than seek status as an architect of community-building.

Communities of various ethnicities, faiths, abilities, genders, and sexualities already engage in meaningful, empowering ways. Our charge is to invite them to see the library as a space worthy of, and open to, their work. Limited cultural competency coaxes program coordinators into amplifying their impact in various communities, especially those not readily seen as "typical" library patrons.

Self-congratulation as a "convener" can overshadow the benefits of collaboration and relationship-building.

When community librarians place their influence alongside the input, and insight, of existing communities, they relinquish the role of "community organizer" for the social currency of "community member."

Well-paced facilitation comforts those who use engagements to atone for attitudes and incidences they've inherited.

The circle, open only to invited guests, becomes a safe zone for questions posed more for relief than response.

- How do I love my grandparents despite their casual, everyday racism?
- What do I do when I see injustice today happening right in front of me?
- How do I raise my white children so they don't become racists?
- How do I raise my Black children so they love themselves?
- What does it mean to love America but despise its history?

These plaintive queries demand a redefinition of the accepted decorum for conversation. Together—participants and library professionals—create "rules of engagement" that prioritize civil disagreement and listening over the protocol of politeness.

Before the conversations about "isms" begin, group members examine the purpose of their gathering.

Invariably, they desire a space for patience, confidentiality, active listening, and no judgment.

"We are not here to play nice," one participant explained. "We've had enough of nice. We are here to be honest."

A VISITOR

She is not happy to be here. Curious, maybe. But not happy like some of our other guests: people eager to enter the library, hear about history, to soften tough words like *segregation* and *Jim Crow* with the tender touch of feel-good memory replayed in past tense.

Instead, she shuffle-steps into the Civil Rights Center, her eyes and forehead tilted toward the carpet. Eighteen stools circle the replica of a lunch counter; she sits in a seat on the outside. And then, at our invitation, she looks up. Her eyes, unblinking behind glasses, jerk across the room slowly, like the second hand of a clock.

This is a special occasion for us—the director of this room dedicated to Nashville's prominent role in the civil rights movement and an associate director of community engagement.

Having elders visit this room—and especially African American elders—amplifies and celebrates the voices of lived experiences.

And right now elders sit in this space where images of exclusion, oppression, struggle, and protest line the walls.

We talk about history; they lived it. We turn history into outreach; they reach out with their stories. But sometimes the reach is wretched, sometimes the stories stir up pain and inspire dialogue that teaches more than history books can attempt.

We welcome the group with emphatic appreciation. Not all memories, we know, come easy.

"We thank you for being here," we tell them. "We are here to hear your stories. To listen more than we speak. We want this to be a day of sharing and teaching."

Some of the elders nod. Our bespectacled guest does not. Finished staring around the room, she sits with about ten women from her senior center, her purse in her lap.

We pose our conversation starter: How does this room make you feel?

"Bad," she says. Our eyes follow her gaze.

TELLING THE WHOLE TRUTH

Every cultural narrative holds tension. Deliberate engagement on topics such as injustice is driven by the kind of personal truth-telling that requires us to loosen our grip on avoiding discontent. Instead, we aim to introduce a social skill that invites the speaker to expose personal biases in safety while the listener absorbs the stories in gratitude.

> In one photo an African American mother escorts two Black girls to first grade amid protesters. The girls look frightened; the mother, serious, with her jaw set in determination. Another photo shows a white woman standing with her arms crossed and her right hip jutted while two women escort a Black boy toward school. It's September 1957, the first day of desegregation in Nashville.
>
> Our guest shakes her head and remembers: "When integration came, the white teachers wouldn't teach me. I didn't learn to read until I was in my thirties. I became the class clown. It was a bad time," she says.
>
> Real bad. School desegregation, she says, was not a celebration for everyone.
>
> For many—the students denied equitable education and the Black teachers who lost their jobs—it is complicated, history with layers of conflict and contradiction.
>
> The quiet that fills the room is the stillness of confirmation and transformation.
>
> How important are conversations that allow personal narratives to expand our understanding of reality? Powerfully important.
>
> What is the impact of community engagement that turns libraries into sanctuaries for vulnerability and truth-telling? Powerful beyond measure.
>
> On this day, we feel the power of this elder's grief. Suspended in midair, right beside our appreciation for her sharing is our recognition that our engagement, our probing has summoned her ghosts.
>
> Is her pain worth this admission? Are we twisting the knife still stuck in her gut?
>
> The collective ache soon finds release. Other elders chime in. They talk about the lost employment, the families torn apart by the comforts of segregation and fear of integration, the toll on Black wealth.
>
> The rest of the group does what thriving communities do when one member has pain: they give her space to push the pain back down. And they pull her back up with words we hear often in the Civil Rights Center: "Lord knows it's not perfect, but look how far we've come."
>
> From there the conversation continues with one eye still glaring at the past, and the other focused on the future.

We take patrons on a journey from uncovering their own story to exploring how their perceptions and cultural identities intersect with the human struggle for freedom and self-definition. Group discussions about such questions as "When was the first time you noticed social injustice?" invite personal memory-mining. Follow-up questions such as "And what was your response?" introduce a conversation that connects the practice of noticing to the cultural norm of bystanding.

So often the answer to these questions is, "I did nothing because I did not know what to do."

Candor, camaraderie, and patience rescue the sharing from shame. What part of our cultural identity guides us toward allyship and community stewardship? Who among us has not witnessed a wrong with a galloping heart, quiet mouth, and frozen knees?

We expand the conversation to exemplify our greatest intention: to encourage participants to view their story as part of a world story, not at the center of it, nor at the margins, but firmly within it.

The method for managing this impact rests not only in humility and disclosure but also in recognizing that we do not get to set the racial agenda for community healing.

Engagement facilitators use their own struggles and missteps to assure patrons of the solid boundaries of their "safe and courageous space." This blended role of participant-facilitator challenges our cultural tendency to respond to awkward discussions with silence and avoidance.

It also derails any attempt to assign an engagement hierarchy in which patrons are positioned as the listeners and library staff become subject experts.

This understanding invites library leaders to step away from the helm of the temple of knowledge and enter the sharing circle. A facilitator may confess about the time she was followed in a store or clutched her purse in an elevator full of Latinx teens or weathered the woes of being a minority in her workplace.

The engagement reveals major differences in worldviews that are challenged publicly and may arouse intense emotions such as dread and anxiety (for whites) and anger and frustration (for people of color).

No matter the narrative, such storytelling legitimizes the engagement as a place of fellowship rather than a space to hear the issues assigned to certain community members.

Facilitators understand and can define racial and cultural identity, can acknowledge and are open to admitting racial biases.

With skills gleaned from our experience as educators, we are equipped with tools to validate and facilitate discussion of feelings; we have techniques to control the process, not the content, of race talk. We are trained to validate, encourage, and express admiration and appreciation to participants who speak when it feels unsafe to do so.

We also admit to carrying the weight of this work ourselves. This emotionally draining, exhaustive work finds release in our ritual debriefing sessions and our gift in finding the comedy in our humanness. As with all jobs, we are tempted to take our psychic residue of our work home and share it with our families. We have learned not to do so. The weight is too heavy.

Instead, we embrace the phenomenon of "facilitator intimacy," where the design, implementation, and review of our work is embedded in using conversation, encouragement, and reflection for self-care.

No matter how powerful the engagement, we, too, must bow to the frailties of our shared humanity. Who can claim themselves impervious to the burdens of racism? Or homophobia? Or ethnocentrism?

Storytelling is deeply rooted in human nature. This is a powerful demonstration of the power that cultural stories have on us. These narratives surround us, making up the subtle cultural background of our communities.

We need to understand which cultural narratives affect our patrons and communities the most. We also need to know how our communities see themselves in relation to that cultural narrative.

Cultural narratives are stories that help a community structure and assign meaning to its history. And libraries are places where diverse communities can gather to share, expand, and examine their own narratives while resisting the urge to own and define agendas and action.

11

STRATEGIC PLANNING THROUGH COMMUNITY LISTENING

AMBER WILLIAMS

L ocated on the easternmost edge of Washington State, Spokane County consists of roughly 1,700 square miles of scenic rivers, lakes, mountains, and plains. In 1942 voters created Spokane County Library District (SCLD) to serve the rural areas outside the city limits of Spokane, which is served by a separate library system. Today, the district's 170-plus employees serve eleven suburban and rural cities and towns in eleven locations. Median household income in Spokane County is 16 percent below the state average, and the values of independence, self-sufficiency, and a pioneering spirit reign—a mindset that, though commendable, can create challenges for libraries wishing to engage all segments of the population.

Serving a region so expansive—by comparison, the state of Rhode Island is about 1,200 square miles—poses unique challenges for a library system. From one library to the next we encounter vastly different community types, population densities, and service priorities. Embracing this community in all its complexities wasn't easy, but former library director Nancy Ledeboer saw it as imperative to the system's growth. "When I first got here [in 2012], I think the mission statement was something like, 'We provide the stuff people want 24/7,'" she said in 2015. "It was very much focused on books and being a popular materials library. If people really want books, they can get them from other places today. If we want support from our communities, we have to show we are focused on caring about our community, not just about books."[1]

Ledeboer began overseeing a systemwide change process when she arrived at the library in 2012. She feared the library was becoming irrelevant as the world continued to change around it. With grant funding through the American Library Association's Libraries Transforming Communities initiative, SCLD staff began working with trainers at the Harwood Institute for Public Innovation to implement Harwood's "turning outward" approach, a community engagement methodology built on the idea that institutions should become symbiotic with their communities by understanding the aspirations of their constituents and helping them achieve those goals.

Within two years, SCLD was operating with a more external focus, and staff were increasingly taking on leadership roles in the community.

Instead of just concentrating on things it was known for in the past—offering popular materials, having good customer service, and being a sound steward of public dollars—the library took steps to work with the community, not just serve the community. Spokane County librarians began serving on local chamber of commerce boards, organizing park cleanups, and joining town revitalization efforts. The community began to see the library as a vital player in addressing issues important to everyone. As a result, the library staff started being asked to partner with other community organizations in deeper ways.[2]

It was a logical progression that when SCLD set out to create a new strategic plan in 2015, the plan was informed by a staff-led listening tour. By integrating community engagement into the strategic planning process, libraries can ensure that the community's goals are baked directly into the library's day-to-day for the duration of the plan, ensuring follow-through and building trust. Staff sought input from the system's 238,000 annual library visitors through community groups, one-on-one conversations with patrons, and online surveys.

Then a librarian in SCLD's Deer Park branch, I was among the first SCLD staff members trained in the community engagement approach. Employing a train-the-trainer model, I then shared what I had learned with fourteen fellow branch librarians so they could learn more about the kind of community their customers wanted and the challenges they saw in making that community a reality. SCLD librarians organized a total of eighty conversations in 2015 in which "residents told the librarians that they felt disconnected from the community; they were concerned about lost jobs and businesses and worried about safety."[3]

That knowledge helped SCLD shape our 2016–2018 Community Engagement Plan and reshape our mission statement: "We build community by connecting people to educational, economic, and recreational opportunities."

THE PROCESS

In 2018, as our existing strategic plan ended, we set out to begin the process anew. With one community engagement–informed planning process under our belt, we knew better this time what to expect. Library staff and leadership had seen the value of the authentic work we had all done over the past three years in response to community wants, and it was an easy decision to inform the new Community Engagement Plan in the same way. The process—which I like to simplify to the three steps of "ask, listen, act"—took place over a nine-month period in 2018.

Month 1: Staff Training

Twenty-two SCLD staff members were invited to a training; all but six had played a role in the 2015 strategic planning process. I kicked off the training with a short history lesson about what we had done before and the successes we had seen across the district because of our community-responsive work. I went over facilitation and notetaker skills, and as a group we practiced the scripts that the trainees would be using in their conversations.

Our questions included these: What kind of community do you want to live in? How is that different than what we have now? What are the barriers keeping us from being the community we want? We broke into small groups to practice, then came back together to discuss strategies and the overall time line for information-gathering and implementation. The six staff members who were new to the process stayed an additional hour to ask questions and identify areas in which they felt they needed more support.

Months 2–7: Listening Tour

Librarians at SCLD had already spent years embedding themselves in their communities by being active in places other than the library. Now, back at their community libraries, they leveraged their new relationships to set up group conversations and one-on-one talks with community members and stakeholders.

Each library was required to complete a minimum of four group conversations and six individual interviews; SCLD staff who worked at the district level spoke to members of boundary-spanning organizations or invited them to participate in conversations. When possible, two staff members were present at the community conversations—one to facilitate the discussion and the other to record notes.

In addition to conducting in-person conversations, we offered the same questions in an online survey, and a self-directed activity placed within the libraries invited patrons to write community aspirations on sticky notes, which were publicly displayed before being gathered for data collection. The goal was to provide multiple arenas through which the people of Spokane County—with their vastly different schedules, investment, and inclinations toward group or solo work—could participate. Overall, we heard from and interacted with several hundred people across the district.

Unsurprisingly, the result was a ton of information. Raw notes were organized into categories: aspirations, challenges, barriers to success, ideas to succeed, and direct quotations.

Month 8: Analyzing Data and Writing Community Reports

After the listening tour was complete, librarians from each location reviewed their notes and identified trends in what they heard. They created a community report for each library location and community served that identified aspirations, concerns, barriers, and a collection of quotes from conversations and interviews that library staff found poignant.

Leveraging the resources we had available to us, we utilized an already scheduled all-staff day to share our progress. Librarians reported their findings to staff who lived and worked in the communities they had conversed with, inviting them to provide feedback and flag any missed issues. This activity was used as a "gut check" to see if what we were hearing from the community resonated with our staff members who worked or lived in those areas. We shared the trends in aspirations, challenges, and barriers and asked staff, "Does this sound right? Are there concerns that you hear about from customers that we didn't hear about?" Finally, librarians adjusted their community reports and submitted them, along with all conversation notes, to a library staff task group charged with writing the Community Engagement Plan.

By this point, SCLD had an overwhelming amount of information about the dreams and wants of the people we serve. Given the district's expansiveness, of course, not all the things we heard were consistent across the county. This inconsistency left us with the task of extrapolating trends. District-level staff and I looked at all the library reports, found trends across the district, and decided which were actionable by using a SOAR (strengths, opportunities, aspirations, results) analysis (see the text box "SOAR Defined" in chapter 4). [4] This tool helped us identify what we did well and what gaps existed in our community that we might be able to fill.

We looked at what we do well, what was a need not being met that was an opportunity for us to try, what we hoped success would look like, and how we would measure success. In the area of opportunities, we looked at community data, such as graduation rates and free and reduced-price lunch percentages, finding ways to tie what we heard from the community to statistics and data, which would later help us with recruiting partners and reporting what we had learned. A challenge in condensing so many individual thoughts and ideas into trends is that you lose the nuance of respondents' actual words. At SCLD we compensated for this loss by collecting direct quotations that gave a level of detail that our broad trends could not.

All this activity informed what we call the *strategic directions* that will guide SCLD's endeavors through 2021. We have strategic priorities based on our core services, values, and the foundations that make a library, but how we implement those priorities is based on our community input-created strategic directions.

After narrowing the strategic directions down to three—engagement, stability, and connectedness (see the accompanying sidebar)—district-level staff and I reported back to the librarians to make sure that they all saw their communities represented in what we had written. Librarians took those three trends, along with their community reports, and reported to community stakeholders to see if our interpretation still rang true with them. Once we had affirmed that what we had written was an authentic representation of our communities' wants and concerns, the first draft of the Community Engagement Plan was ready to send to the board of trustees for approval and implementation.

SPOKANE COUNTY LIBRARY DISTRICT: 2019–2021 COMMUNITY ACTION PLAN

The following three strategic directions inform district decisions and provide direction for our four strategic priorities: Early Learning, Business and Career Development, Education and Enrichment, and Digital Interaction and Sharing.

Engagement: People desire a sense of belonging in their community where individuals matter to one another and everyone feels pride in the community where we live.

Stability: Residents long for physical and emotional needs to be met. These needs include food and shelter, safety within the community outside library walls, and economic security for individuals and the region as a whole.

Connectedness: Families and individuals of all ages wish to participate in entertaining events and activities that are affordable and close to home.

Month 9: Presenting to the Board

I presented the resulting 2019–2021 Community Action Plan to the SCLD Board of Trustees. Part of that presentation was an overview of the process, including why we structured the process as we did and who was involved.

TIME FOR ACTION

At that point, it was time to put what we had learned into practice. We were in the final stage of "ask, listen, act."

Often, the result of our action plan was a new program or service. For example, during our 2018 round of community conversations, SCLD heard in many different ways about residents' desire for stability in their lives. Sometimes it was economic stability, other times it was mental health, and often it was the desire to meet basic human needs. This theme was especially prominent in the city of Spokane Valley, which houses a library branch. One resident stated, "If we can help a generation properly, we'll see the difference in our lifetime." With this goal in mind, Managing Librarian Aileen Luppert used the successful partnerships she had gained in her years of being out of the building to address summer access to food.

During the 2016–17 school year, 851 high school students from four local school districts were identified as homeless; it is believed that the number has gone up since the last formal count.[5] Working with partnering organizations, Luppert volunteered the Spokane Valley library, of which she is the manager, as a pickup point for emergency groceries. Young people can now come in all summer and have access to shelf-stable items. It's the perfect place because the library is open and staffed seven days a week with much longer hours than any of the other nonprofit partners making the endeavor happen.

TAKEAWAYS

Having been through this strategic planning process twice, I can see how far we've come. Here are some of the most important lessons I have learned.

The Process Is Flexible

In our first Community Engagement Planning process in 2015, we strictly followed the parameters set by the Harwood Institute for Public Innovation.

These guidelines recommend asking questions in a variety of formats, including brief, one-on-one interviews; invited, ninety-minute facilitated conversations; and staff insight sessions. We conducted the recommended number of conversations and used the tools provided to decipher our next steps. Some of these pieces worked for us; others didn't.

The second time around, we adapted what worked best for us. For SCLD, the ninety-minute conversations felt too long, and we had difficulty recruiting participants for such a lengthy sit-down talk. So we shortened those community conversations to sixty minutes and focused them on the three main questions: What kind of community do you want to live in? How is that different than what we have now? What are the barriers keeping us from being the community we want? We talked to more people via a five-minute interview model at library and community events. By focusing on just three areas, we were able to stay focused and succinct. We learned that community engagement doesn't mean following a recipe step by step. If you stay within the broad steps—ask, listen, act—there is infinite room for interpretation and personalization.

Other libraries, of course, have tackled this process in different ways. Mary Lou Willits was new to the director position at Pawlet (Vermont) Public Library when she suggested that the board of trustees consider a new way to develop their next strategic plan. The Pawlet Public Library is small, serving 1,350 residents with a two-person staff, so when Willits wanted to ask Pawlet community members about their aspirations to inform the library's next strategic plan, she had to start by recruiting help to do so. Two trustees and three community members joined Willits in speaking to thirteen community groups. They asked these three questions:

1. What are your aspirations for your community?
2. What challenges do you face in reaching these aspirations?
3. What changes are needed in your community to reach your aspirations?

The library heard from community members that they wanted to "bring people together and bridge community divisions." Willits built momentum on the positive buzz the strategic planning process created and started offering community potlucks and new programs for different ages, including square dancing, canning fruit, and learning how to fish.

From what they heard, planning group participants created top-ten lists for aspirations, challenges, and changes and used those lists to inform their strategic plan. When they unveiled the new plan, forty-five community members attended the event. About the experience, Willits said, "Have confidence that community engagement will catapult your library's purpose and build community support. If you put in the time and hard work it requires to do engaged strategic planning, you will have a clear road map for implementation." (Read the Pawlet Public Library's strategic plan at https://pawletpubliclibrary .wordpress.com/strategic-plan/.)

Know That the Process Takes Time

Although the process is flexible, it is a large undertaking, and participating staff need to commit to the time and resources it demands. The listening tour is an especially heavy lift. But all this work has value. In addition to collecting information for a strategic plan, you are raising your library's profile by being out in the community and meeting new audiences who may not yet use library services.

You Can't Do Everything

Libraries' resources are limited. Not everything you hear needs to translate into a library program, library-led event, or strategic direction. You've shifted culture, you've raised your community profile, and everyone wants to work with you because you've been so good at saying yes—but it's unrealistic to think your library can do it all.

Community engagement work is not sustainable if you cannot keep up with the workload. Overcommitment will lead to burnout, turnover, broken promises, and community distrust.

Sustaining this work doesn't just mean direct action; often it means simple follow-through, such as a well-placed phone call. When your community complains about potholes, don't think you and your staff need to learn how to spread asphalt. You do need to act on what you hear; in this case, the action is reporting the problem to the proper local government office. In Deer Park I heard about a dangerous intersection commonly called "coffin corner." I was able to report the concern to the Washington State Department of Transportation and learned it was already on their radar. Now, coffin corner no longer has corners—it has become a roundabout.

Another valuable skill is using your newfound knowledge of the community to play matchmaker. When a potential partner approaches you with a project idea, consider who else might be a more appropriate partner. The important thing is to keep the exchange positive—and to keep the ball in the potential partner's court. (One of my go-to responses is, "That's an amazing idea! What can the library do to help you make it happen?")

Failure Can Be a Gift

Although most of us will go to great lengths to avoid failure, it is only through trying and failing that we can learn—and clear some of the less useful projects from our slate. In summer 2015 SCLD responded to the community-identified aspirations to have opportunities to meet across generations, provide tech help for seniors, and develop job marketable skills for teens by introducing a program that recruited teen volunteers to give device help to seniors at the library. It was a failure: not a single senior signed up, and not a single teen volunteered. We decided to cancel the program and move on, knowing more about our community members and their wants than we did before.

We eventually found success by taking work we were already doing and using the lens of the community's aspirations to adjust. In this case it meant looking at programs we were already planning and tweaking them to be more family- and all-ages–friendly. A painting class for kids became a painting class for families; a music concert in the meeting room became a music program in the parks. Participation and attendance went up.

We also implemented a temporary employment opportunity for high school students to work in the library in the summer. Students in these positions work with camera equipment and editing software, leading programs for their peers and offering one-on-one assistance for patrons of all ages. Although it was difficult to find volunteers, we have had no shortage of applications for a paid position. After hearing in the 2018 round of conversations so much about job and economic stability, we expanded the student positions by offering three more opportunities during the school year and opening the summer positions to all ages.

You'll Be Doing This Again and Again . . . but It Gets Easier

Community engagement is not a one-and-done situation. It is cyclical, and if done well the cycle looks a bit different each time around. Being adaptable to change means staying responsive and flexible. We want to change our communities, and we'll need to change with them.

Getting people to talk to us in 2015 about their community aspirations felt harder than pulling teeth. It was a challenge, and it took many of our staff outside their comfort zone. Going back out in 2018, those same staff members who had struggled (myself included) found it much easier because of the relationships we had cultivated over the preceding three years. As the Deer Park community librarian in 2018, I could cold-call the mayor of Deer Park and ask for fifteen minutes of his time to talk about where he hoped Deer Park was headed. I could even make this call comfortably.

NOTES

1. American Library Association, "Libraries Transforming Communities Case Studies" (Chicago: American Library Association, 2016), 16, www.ala.org/tools/sites/ala.org.tools/files/content/LTC-case-studies-complete.pdf.

2. American Library Association, "Libraries Transforming Communities Case Studies," 15.

3. American Library Association, "Libraries Transforming Communities Case Studies," 16.

4. Aspen Institute, *Action Guide for Re-Envisioning Your Public Library, Version 2.0* (Washington, DC: Aspen Institute, 2017), 20, csreports.aspeninstitute.org/documents/ActionGuideFINAL_7_12_17.pdf.

5. Washington Office of Superintendent of Public Instruction, "Homeless Education Student Data," www.k12.wa.us/homeless-education-student-data.

BUILDING PUBLIC TRUST

It Starts with the Individual

Every library has its own public, or community, made up of people it has committed to serving. Striving to understand our communities and build inclusive, equitable relationships is essential to earning the confidence and support of our communities. Relationships like these, based on honest and authentic communication, help increase the impact of libraries on our campuses and throughout our cities, schools, and offices.

But how do we build these authentic relationships? How do we learn to trust ourselves, to develop the confidence needed to reach out? How do librarians find the courage to seek out and listen to marginalized groups who have yet to be heard? What guides the individual library faculty or staff member and urges that individual to develop good judgment and personal strength?

These are important questions because it is these individuals who make up our library teams. It is the public service librarian, the information literacy specialist, the programming coordinator, and others like them who come together to evolve and sustain the library's culture of engagement. It is those teams of sensitive and engaged staff members who will build deep and lasting relationships with community partners. As critical as it is to build mutually beneficial relationships with stakeholders, valuing the individual and modeling ethical behavior are essential to developing the teams that libraries need to engage effectively with their public.

To help address the ongoing need to find solutions, reach shared goals, and ultimately build public trust, this chapter will look closely at three engagement ideas that stand out for their timely focus. We will look back to the fourth century BC to the principles of the great philosopher Aristotle and his exploration of *Practical Wisdom*. We will then jump to two contemporary authors—Richard Harwood and his discussion of *Civic Faith*, and Kathleen Fitzpatrick and her examination of *Generous Thinking*.

Each of these scholars strongly advocates for the power and necessity of community. They agree that, for communities to thrive, individuals must practice and develop their engagement skills; they must hone their ability to make sound decisions for the good of the greater collective. Although not targeted specifically to librarians, the teachings of Aristotle and the later writings of Harwood and Fitzpatrick speak directly to faculty and staff working at all levels of every library, urging them to embrace their individual virtues and strengths and recognize their obligation to the public good.

Ours is a profession of sensitivity and integrity. Librarians are trained relationship builders. We build collections, develop programs, and fulfill information needs based on the desires of our constituents. Success in this role means that librarians must be empathic listeners. We need to be curious, ask questions, build networks, and make connections. We must recognize and develop our individual strengths and responsibilities, as Aristotle, Harwood, and Fitzpatrick emphasize, and work together to strengthen the library culture and ensure that libraries remain the relevant, foundational institutions that our communities need.

EMBRACING PUBLIC TRUST

Each time we pass through our public spaces, the question presents as a gentle nudge against an unconscious reliance on public trust. Would you, could you, should you trust?

—CLAUDIA RANKINE[1]

Should we trust? Can we expect others to trust us? This is a very personal consideration. Trust draws on our individual experiences and tangible knowledge. At the same time, it is based on belief and on hope. Trust can be lost and, once lost, can be hard to regain. Earning the trust of another person can be a complex task. Among other qualities, one needs to demonstrate character traits such as dependability and truthfulness. A trustworthy individual is considered reliable; we feel confidence in that person's conviction, ability, competence, and inherent worth.

For every type of library, public trust happens when the diverse, individual members of the community collectively come to believe in and support their

WHAT IS "THE PUBLIC"?

In its 2019 National Impact of Library Public Programs Assessment report, the American Library Association determined a library's public to be "the community the library serves or the audiences the library targets with its programs. For example, for a public library, the audience may consist of the whole community or a component of the community, such as older adults. In the case of the academic library, the public may be the student body, a specific department, or a special component of students."[1]

NOTE
1. B. Sheppard, K. Flinner, R. J. Norlander, and M. D. Fournier, *National Impact of Library Public Programs Assessment, Phase 1: A White Paper on the Dimensions of Library Programs and the Skills and Training for Library Program Professionals*, NewKnowledge Publication #IML.074.207.07 (Chicago: American Library Association and New Knowledge Organization, 2019), 7, https://nilppa.org/.

library professionals, facilities, and services. Libraries serve a broad range of the human spectrum: learners of all ages, researchers, corporate professionals, students, and teachers—information seekers of every ilk.

Recent studies by the Pew Research Center and the Maine State Library conclude that libraries continue to be considered trusted institutions by their many constituents. The Pew Center's 2016 study found that "most Americans view public libraries as important parts of their communities, with a majority reporting that libraries have the resources they need and play at least some role in helping them decide what information they can trust."[2] The Maine State Library's 2016 Trusted Professionals Survey measured the perceived "trustworthiness" (honest and ethical standards) of twenty-two professions in the state of Maine and found the top rated to be nurses (81 percent), followed by librarians (78 percent).[3]

As twenty-first-century challenges mount, libraries look to their public to guide future strategies and directions and to provide much-needed support. At the same time, community members turn to their libraries to voice concerns and share aspirations—to be heard and acknowledged. With a growing scarcity of resources and an increasing need to engage with stakeholders, the time is right for libraries to focus on leveraging the personal strengths of staff members, encouraging them to make connections, welcome new ideas, and recognize the library culture as one of sensitive engagement and hope.

Libraries can build trust within their walls and throughout their communities by creating a culture in which empathy is expected, community experience is respected, and rich engagement with the community is rewarded.

ENGAGEMENT IDEAS

Now we turn to three scholarly perspectives on strengthening communities, beginning with the earliest in the fourth century BC.

Practical Wisdom

Practical wisdom combines the will to do the right thing with the skill to figure out what the right thing is.

—BARRY SCHWARTZ AND KENNETH SHARPE[4]

Aristotle, prolific writer, teacher, and philosopher of ancient Greece, believed strongly in the value of community. Aristotle felt that human beings derived their identity and moral purpose from their participation in an existing community—the world of parents, ancestors, friends, customs, institutions, and laws. In Book VI of his classic monograph, *Nicomachean Ethics,* Aristotle discussed intellectual virtues and delved deeply into the idea of Practical Wisdom, a virtue acquired through experience and daily living and a necessary guide to personal and communal well-being.[5]

In their book *Practical Wisdom: The Right Way to Do the Right Thing*, authors Barry Schwartz and Kenneth Sharpe say, "Character and practical wisdom must be cultivated by the major institutions in which we practice."[6]

It was Aristotle's belief that for human beings to live and flourish in community with one another, they must always be developing their inner selves. He believed that people must learn and practice character virtues such as loyalty, fairness, truthfulness, and generosity every day. They must use their personal knowledge and experience, their practical wisdom, to guide them in the use of these virtues.

As in the fourth century BC, practical wisdom continues to guide us today as we work to identify and reduce barriers and reach goals. Practical wisdom is gained through lived experience and the development of personal knowledge. As librarians, we use it as we confront the social justice issues facing our communities and our institutions. It helps us make informed choices as we address budget shortfalls and diminishing resources. We are gaining practical wisdom by listening to and engaging with community members, and, by working together in community, we can develop well-considered and pertinent collections, services, and programs.

A modern-day example of practical wisdom working in libraries can be seen in the ongoing debate about overdue fines on children's materials. Should they be collected or forgiven? It is a current conversation in public libraries across the country, and it is a discussion, it can be argued, fueled by practical wisdom.

As librarians watch dozens of books go home with scores of children each day, they know that when the due date arrives, some of those books will be unaccounted for. Their own knowledge and experience may tell them that this loss is inevitable and that by eliminating fines they can maintain goodwill with families and keep them returning to the library. That said, librarians also understand that the money collected in overdue fines helps fund important programming and collection-building that otherwise might not take place. Collected fines add significantly to operating budgets. The final decision can be guided by the practical wisdom found in and encouraged by local library staff members who understand the needs of their community.

Schwartz and Sharpe grapple with Aristotle's writings and help us put his ideas into our current context. The authors offer six key characteristics of a practically wise person, listed here in an abbreviated form:

1. A wise person knows the proper aims of the activity she is engaged in.
2. A wise person knows how to improvise.
3. A wise person is perceptive and knows how to read a social context.
4. A wise person knows how to take on the perspective of another.
5. A wise person knows how to make emotion an ally of reason.
6. A wise person is an experienced person.[7]

Librarians earn the trust of their public by demonstrating these traits when tackling complex issues. In the case of overdue fines, a practically wise librarian knows that collecting fines on children's books is not a clear-cut issue. Collecting or forgiving fines impacts library stakeholders in different ways. Librarians know that there may be times when improvising, or even breaking the rules, is called for. A wise librarian understands that communities are strengthened by the multiple differences represented within the collective. Library professionals use their lived experiences, seek out varying perspectives, and bring voices together to identify shared goals and potential actions.

Cultivating, encouraging, and rewarding practical wisdom allows library professionals to sustain close and satisfying relations with each other and with people throughout their communities. As Schwartz and Sharpe have determined, "Wise practitioners improve not only the lives of the people they serve; they improve their own lives as well."[8]

Civic Faith

We can't get there on our own, doing it by ourselves.

—RICHARD HARWOOD[9]

Fast-forward about 2,300 years to 1988. That is when Richard Harwood, founder of the Harwood Institute, was beginning to put his thoughts together about the idea of civic faith. Civic faith is a philosophy that places people, community, and shared responsibility at the center of healthy and hopeful societies. Civic faith supports the idea that human beings have an innate capacity to shape their own lives as well as the lives they share with others. Civic faith advocates the beliefs that community is a common enterprise and that only by working together can we create the productive, supportive relationships needed to strengthen our communities and forge a stronger common good.

If we are encouraged to bring our knowledge and unique life experiences to the table and, together, seek solutions and new directions for engagement, seeds will be planted and new answers will likely be found. Our collective strength as a library team can then spark change. Civic faith urges us to listen to one another and to seek, share, and respect the perspectives of our public—to recognize their wisdom. Nurturing a belief in the inherent value of people and their perspectives motivates us, as individuals, to contribute to the common good, to be part of the solution.

Several figures throughout history have advocated for the sensibilities surrounding civic faith. A short list of influential people identified by Richard Harwood includes Abraham Lincoln, Walt Whitman, Eleanor Roosevelt, Ralph Ellison, and Dorothy Day. Their words speak of self-reliance and self-trust. They celebrate human potential, and they advocate for collective action.[10]

In his book *Stepping Forward: A Positive, Practical Path to Transform Our Communities and Our Lives*, Harwood expands on the idea that individuals and institutions share responsibility when it comes to strengthening communities and building public trust. "There is something basic—radical—at the core of shared responsibility: it is relational. Shared responsibility is rooted in a covenant of sorts—an agreement between and among people that reflects a common purpose, infused by shared obligations, undertaken entirely by one's own will. Like all covenants, it calls us to be part of something larger than ourselves, in service to something that includes, yet transcends, ourselves."[11]

"At the heart of this civic faith are people," Harwood writes. "People must always be at the center of what we do—their lives, what matters to them, their aspirations."[12]

Harwood encourages us to consider two important points when thinking about public trust and how to earn it:

1. [There is] a deep yearning among people to be part of something larger than themselves. . . . We long to build things together and want to be more connected and engaged. . . .
2. Solutions to many of our current challenges require marshaling our shared resources. . . . No single organization, no one leader or group of citizens can tackle these problems on their own.[13]

Emilie Hancock, adult services generalist for the Charleston County (South Carolina) Public Library (CCPL), illustrates the idea of civic faith in her description of a conversation series implemented in her library that was designed to help community members talk about divisive issues. She sought feedback from both library colleagues and community members and was rewarded with enthusiastic participation. "I received such wonderful, positive feedback from everyone—potential participants, actual participants, library colleagues, peers and professors, friends—you name it! There were new words, new perspectives, new theories. It was awesome. Everyone also said it helped them feel closer to each other, and they hope to continue to talk to each other over time."[14]

The community conversation series at CCPL succeeded in building the rich relationships that support public trust. The library's staff members were given an opportunity to embrace their yearning for genuine engagement and to use that yearning to find collective solutions with their fellow community members.

Generous Thinking

Our common presence in a space, an institution, a community, obligates us to one another.

—KATHLEEN FITZPATRICK[15]

Building and sustaining public trust is a goal shared by all libraries, and academic libraries are no exception. In her book *Generous Thinking: A Radical Approach to Saving the University*, Kathleen Fitzpatrick, digital humanities director and professor of English at Michigan State University, takes a new but not unfamiliar look at engaging our public—those found inside and outside our institutions. Fitzpatrick sheds new light on our need to build constructive relationships with our colleagues. She then suggests ways to use our acquired wisdom to listen to our community members, to hear their stories, and, equally important, to help them understand our story.

Fitzpatrick introduces a new concept—generous thinking—"a mode of engagement that emphasizes listening over speaking, community over individualism, collaboration over competition and lingering with the ideas that are in front of us rather than continually pressing forward to where we want to go."[16] Although Fitzpatrick was writing with the university in mind, her insights and considerations speak to all of us and help us think about public confidence and trust in a new way.

"To listen is to be ready for that which one has not yet heard—and, in fact, for that which one might not yet be willing or able to hear," Fitzpatrick writes.[17]

At the root of Fitzpatrick's thoughts surrounding generous thinking is a word that resonates: *obligation*. *Obligation* is a term that is nonnegotiable. It is undeniable. Fitzpatrick considers it something that "binds us together, that which we cannot walk away from without doing grave things both to ourselves and the fabric of the whole."[18]

Adding a sense of obligation to the list of criteria necessary for authentic, effective engagement helps us understand that we cannot, on our own, solve the obstacles we face. Emphasizing generous thinking in our libraries helps build a collective of sensitive, responsive, and collaborative staff members—professionals who are committed to listening, taking action, and earning the trust of their public.

Librarians are well placed to advance the idea of generous thinking. We are relationship builders, we collaborate with our campus and community colleagues, and we work to increase public access to both analog and digital materials. On an increasing number of college and university campuses, compassionate communication workshops are being offered as a way to help faculty and staff deepen their relationships and enhance their communication skills. This type of training helps employees at every level recognize and strengthen their skills as generous thinkers and harness their interest in authentic engagement. It supports an institutional culture in which generosity can be practiced and rewarded, shared responsibility understood, and different perspectives sought and considered. As individual librarians develop their engagement skills, the overall impact of the library increases, and the library's status as the trusted "heart of the university" remains in place.

PUBLIC TRUST AND RETURN ON INVESTMENT

As stated earlier, public trust is achieved when the diverse, individual members of the community collectively come to believe in and support their library's staff members, facilities, and services. The actual return on investment (ROI) that results from this confidence and trust, however, is not always easy to measure. Library administrators are looking for both economic and social ROIs. In a survey on libraries and community engagement, ALA questioned library staff members about their community engagement successes. When asked about lasting impacts resulting from their work, respondents shared the following:

- Relationships were strengthened.
- Friendships were created.
- Awareness and use of the library increased.
- Excitement was generated around library services.

Respondents spoke of specific outcomes, such as a stronger library presence developed in underutilized neighborhoods, more diversity seen in the library, an increased understanding of library value, and programming and planning in the library that continued to grow and evolve due to community input. Sara McGough, manager of the Ben May Main Library at Mobile (Alabama) Public Library, shared that "friends were made and networking took place. Wisdom was shared, which allowed people to get a better understanding of all they experienced and/or heard. More customers now frequent the library."[19]

This feedback supports the idea that practical wisdom, generated in our libraries and then practiced and shared throughout our communities, creates the goodwill and constituent satisfaction that increase public trust.

Cultivating an engaged culture within libraries is a significant strategic decision, and many factors must be taken into consideration. Creating an environment in which staff members are provided regular opportunities and encouragement to contribute their talents, share their stories, listen, and be heard requires support at every level of the library. Honest, cooperative, and well-considered thought-processes and strategies, embedded in our libraries and practiced throughout our communities, help improve employee morale and confidence.

Relationships between the library and community, enriched through effective engagement, can lead to supplemental funds gained through collaborative grant awards and partnerships. Fund-raising efforts and planned giving campaigns, sponsored by advocate groups and Friends of the Library, will benefit from stories told about a supportive and flourishing library environment.

"Our talented faculty and staff deserve appreciation for and investment in their unique talents. They are enterprising, courageous, devoted, passionate, and creative. This plan calls on them to be even more agile, experimental, and open to the unknown. We will support and retain talented individuals committed to the public good through timely, continuous, and multi-faceted opportunities for professional development. We aim to be the exemplar on campus, a place that others can learn from as we pave the way," says the University of Denver's 2018–2025 Keystone Strategic Plan for the College of Arts, Humanities, and Social Sciences (https://liberalarts.du.edu/sites/g/files/lmucqz471/files/2019 -08/keystonestrategicplan.pdf).

LOOKING FORWARD

So where does this leave us? ALA's Core Values of Librarianship state that the "foundation of modern librarianship rests on an essential set of core values that define, inform, and guide our professional practice. These values reflect the history and ongoing development of the profession and have been advanced, expanded, and refined by numerous policy statements of the American Library Association. Among these are: access, confidentiality/privacy, democracy, diversity, education and lifelong learning, intellectual freedom, preservation, the public good, professionalism, service, social responsibility, and sustainability."[20]

The Core Values outline the principles that form the foundation of library culture. This overriding commitment to the greater good is what makes the library one of the most trusted institutions in our country and the field of librarianship one of the most trusted professions. In their chapter "Justifying Professional Education in a Self-Service World," authors Rachel Rubin and Richard Rubin say this about the Core Values: "To ignore these fundamental values would render our profession without a compass."[21]

Of course, it is not only library professionals who are driven by their sense of obligation and their commitment to the common good. Professionals from multiple disciplines, institutions, and perspectives focus their attention on building trust. The human belief that one can transform societies for the greater good is what propels many individuals to enter fields in which they can use their personal strengths to guide and empower others. Institutions are obliged to nurture and utilize the passion and energy that individuals bring to their positions and use their momentum to strengthen communities and identify solutions. As Kathleen Fitzpatrick wrote, "Those of us who work in institutions must take a good hard look at ourselves and the way that we engage with one another and with the world, in order to ensure that we're doing everything we possibly can to create the ways of thinking we'd like to see manifested around us."[22]

Aristotle, Harwood, and Fitzpatrick help us understand that we have the capacity and the ability inside each of us to address the issues that confront us. And it is up to us, as individuals, to reach out with tolerance and compassion and build strong communities.

- Aristotle spoke of practical wisdom as the guide to developing individual moral strengths—character traits essential to flourishing in community with others.
- Richard Harwood describes civic faith as a civic covenant. "We are in relationship with one another," he says, "and that is the only way a shared society works."

- Kathleen Fitzpatrick urges generous thinking, based on an individual sense of obligation that "binds us together."

All three scholars send an impassioned reminder to individuals and institutions that, for communities to thrive and for trust to be earned, different voices and perspectives must come together. We must learn from one another, share our stories, and build strong, healthy collectives that, together, can solve common problems and reach shared goals.

· · · · · ·

The greatness of a community is most accurately measured by the compassionate actions of its members.

—CORETTA SCOTT KING[23]

NOTES

1. Claudia Rankine, "Public Trust: Script for Situation Video," *RSA Journal,* 26 (2015).
2. Pew Center for Research, *Libraries* (Washington, DC: Pew Center, 2016).
3. Portland Research Group, Maine State Library, Bruce M. Lockwood, and James Ritter, "Maine State Library: Trusted Professionals Survey 2016," *Library Documents* (2016), https://digitalmaine.com/msl_docs/101.
4. Barry Schwartz and Kenneth Sharpe, *Practical Wisdom: The Right Way to Do the Right Thing* (New York: Riverhead Books, 2010).
5. Ian Johnston, lecture delivered, in part, in Liberal Studies 301 on November 18, 1997, at Malaspina College (now Vancouver Island University). This document is in the Public Domain, and may be used by anyone, in whole or in part, without permission and without charge, provided the source is acknowledged; released November 1997; revised slightly in April 2014.
6. Schwartz and Sharpe, *Practical Wisdom.*
7. Schwartz and Sharpe, *Practical Wisdom.*
8. Schwartz and Sharpe, *Practical Wisdom.*
9. Richard C. Harwood, *Stepping Forward: A Positive, Practical Path to Transform Our Communities and Our Lives* (Austin, TX: Greenleaf Book Group Press, 2019).
10. Harwood, *Stepping Forward.*
11. Harwood, *Stepping Forward.*
12. Harwood, *Stepping Forward.*
13. Harwood, *Stepping Forward.*
14. American Library Association, "Empowering Communities: The Library and Community Engagement Survey" (Chicago: American Library Association, 2019).
15. Kathleen Fitzpatrick, *Generous Thinking: A Radical Approach to Saving the University* (Baltimore: Johns Hopkins University Press, 2019).

16. Fitzpatrick, *Generous Thinking*.

17. Fitzpatrick, *Generous Thinking*.

18. Fitzpatrick, *Generous Thinking*.

19. American Library Association, "Empowering Communities."

20. American Library Association, "Core Values of Librarianship" (adopted January 2019), www.ala.org/advocacy/intfreedom/corevalues.

21. Rachel Rubin and Richard Rubin, "Justifying Professional Education in a Self-Service World," in *Defending Professionalism: A Resource for Librarians, Information Specialists, Knowledge Managers, and Archivists*, edited by Bill Crowley (Santa Barbara, CA: Libraries Unlimited, 2012), 27.

22. Fitzpatrick, *Generous Thinking*.

23. "King's Widow Urges Acts of Compassion," *Los Angeles Times*, January 17, 2000, https://www.latimes.com/archives/la-xpm-2000-jan-17-mn-54832-story.html.

RESOURCES

Libraries Transforming Communities (ala.org/LTC). Since 2014 the American Library Association's Public Programs Office has assembled a wide variety of tools and approaches and invested in numerous professional development opportunities to "strengthen libraries' role as core community leaders and change agents. The initiative addresses a critical need within the library field by developing and distributing new tools, resources, and support for librarians to engage with their communities in new ways." Information and tools are organized into categories for large public libraries, academic libraries, and small and rural libraries.

Communities + Libraries (C+L; https://sites.google.com/view/cplusl/home). This model addresses the question, What skills does an information professional in any position at any library type in any community need to help that community be a better place? Designed as a yearlong, cohort-based learning process, C+L works with libraries and community partners to identify and address community aspirations while taking stock of all available assets, building capacity through strategic partnerships, and creating space for all voices at the decision-making table. The process brings together community engagement, sustainability, regenerative development, asset-based community development, social justice, and community organizing to create thriving communities.

Community-Led Libraries Toolkit (https://www.vpl.ca/sites/vpl/public/ Community-Led-Libraries-Toolkit.pdf). Developed by the Vancouver Public Library, this toolkit was a product of the Working Together Project. The toolkit takes a community development approach to using library skills to work collaboratively with the community to address its needs while identifying systemic barriers to library use for socially excluded people. It provides examples of policy and procedural changes, staff development, and evaluation, as well as an inclusive service planning model, to address these barriers.

National Coalition for Dialogue and Deliberation (www.ncdd.org). The National Coalition for Dialogue and Deliberation (NCDD) is a network of innovators who bring people together across divides to tackle today's toughest challenges. NCDD serves as a gathering place, a resource clearinghouse, a news source, and a facilitative leader for this extraordinary community.

- **NCDD Resource Center, Beginner's Guide** (www.ncdd.org/rc/ beginners-guide/). The National Coalition for Dialogue and Deliberation's resource center includes more than 3,100 resources from the field of dialogue and deliberation. The best starting point for new facilitators is the Beginner's Guide, which features the very best resources for those getting started.
- **NCDD Resource Center, Engagement Streams Framework** (www .ncdd.org/streams). The Engagement Steams Framework helps you navigate the range of dialogue and deliberation approaches available so you can select the right one for your situation. This reference includes a chart of approaches with information on the time needed, number of participants, expected outcomes, and more.
- **NCDD Resource Center, Manuals and Guides** (www.ncdd.org/ rc/?category_name=manuals-guides&tag=highly-recommended). NCDD has collected some of the best how-to manuals and guidebooks for various topics. Not sure where to start in planning for a conversation? Peruse these materials to explore your options.

World Café, *The Art of Powerful Questions* (www.theworldcafe.com/ tools-store/store/). "This comprehensive guide written by Eric Vogt, Juanita Brown, and David Isaacs explores the three dimensions of a powerful question—construction, scope, and assumptions—and then offers sample questions for focusing collective attention, finding deeper insight, and creating forward movement."

TOOLS AND RESOURCES FOR UNDERSTANDING AND INCREASING EQUITY

- **ALA's Office for Diversity, Literacy and Outreach Services** (ODLOS; www.ala.org/diversity). ODLOS supports library and information science workers in creating responsible and all-inclusive spaces that serve and represent the entire community. To accomplish this, ODLOS decenters power and privilege by facilitating conversations about access and identity as they impact the profession and those we serve. ODLOS uses a social justice framework to inform library and information science workers' development of resources. ODLOS strives to create an association culture in which these concerns are incorporated into everybody's everyday work.
- **ALA's Libraries Respond: Black Lives Matter** (www.ala.org/ advocacy/diversity/librariesrespond/black-lives-matter). The profession of librarianship suffers from a persistent lack of racial and ethnic diversity that shows few signs of improving. ALA offers ways we can center the voices and experiences of Black library workers and the black community, support the broader Black Lives Matter movement, fight against police violence, and help the cause of racial justice.
- **Center for Story-Based Strategy, "The 4th Box"** (https://www.story basedstrategy.org/tools-and-resources#the-4th-box-resources)
- **Government Alliance on Race and Equity,** *Racial Equity Toolkit: An Opportunity to Operationalize Equity* (http://www.racialequity alliance.org/resources/racial-equity-toolkit-opportunity -operationalize-equity/)
- **Peggy McIntosh, "White Privilege: Unpacking the Invisible Knapsack"** and **"Some Notes for Facilitators"** (https://nationalseed project.org/Key-SEED-Texts/white-privilege-unpacking-the -invisible-knapsack
- **Seattle Office for Civil Rights,** *Inclusive Outreach and Public Engagement Guide* (https://www.seattle.gov/Documents/Departments/ ParksAndRecreation/Business/RFPs/Attachment5%20_Inclusive OutreachandPublicEngagement.pdf)
- **Simmons University Library, Anti-Oppression LibGuide** (https://simmons.libguides.com/anti-oppression)

DIALOGUE AND DELIBERATION MODELS

Conversation Cafés are open, hosted conversations in cafés as well as conferences and classrooms—anywhere people gather to make sense of our world. At a Conversation Café there is nothing to join, no homework, no agenda, just a simple process that helps to shift us from small talk to BIG talk, conversations that matter. It is a ninety-minute hosted conversation, held in a public setting like a café, where anyone is welcome to join. A simple format helps people feel at ease and gives everyone who wants it a chance to speak—it's also fine for people to simply listen.

Use Conversation Café when: You want participants to learn more about themselves, their community, or an issue, and to discover innovative solutions to problems.

Topics suited for this model: Nearly anything! It is particularly suited for exploring topics (e.g., community, love, death) or for processing events or issues, such as instances of violence or other crises in a community.

Essential Partners' Reflective Structured Dialogue method helps people with fundamental disagreements about divisive issues develop the mutual understanding and trust essential for strong communities and positive action. It draws on strategies developed by family therapists to promote effective communication in the midst of painful differences. The method also incorporates insights and tools from mediation, interpersonal communications, appreciative inquiry, organization development, and psychology and neurobiology.

The model is characterized by a careful preparatory phase in which all stakeholders or sides are interviewed and prepared for the dialogue process. This approach enables participants to share experiences and explore questions that both clarify their own perspectives and help them become more comfortable around, and curious about, those with whom they are in conflict.

Use Essential Partners' Reflective Structured Dialogue method when: There is a need to resolve conflicts, encourage community healing after a crisis or trauma, or improve relations among groups in your community.

Topics suited for this process: Political polarization, Jewish-Muslim relations, race relations, and other value-based conflicts.

Everyday Democracy's Dialogue to Change process encourages diverse groups of people to come together, engage in inclusive and respectful dialogue, and find common solutions to community problems. Everyday Democracy's process is suited for communities that want to build trust, relationships, and collaboration among residents and that want to examine issues of institutional racism and socioeconomic and other disparities.

The dialogues consist of groups of eight to ten people from different backgrounds and viewpoints who meet several times to talk about an issue. These community dialogues create spaces in which everyone has an equal voice and people try to understand each other's views. They do not have to always agree with each other. The idea is to share concerns and look for ways to make things better. In its Dialogue to Change process, Everyday Democracy places a great deal of importance on using a "racial equity lens" at every stage of the process to ensure inclusiveness and guarantee that outcomes do not perpetuate or create new disparities but, rather, remove existing ones.

A trained facilitator drawn from the community helps the group focus on different views and makes sure that the discussion goes well and that participants contribute action ideas. In a large-scale (or community-wide) dialogue program, people all over a neighborhood, city, county, school district, or region participate in such dialogues over the same period. At the end of the dialogue rounds, participants come together in a large community meeting to work together on the action ideas that emerged from the dialogues.

Use Everyday Democracy's Dialogue to Change process when: There is a need or desire to empower community members to solve complicated problems and take responsibility for the solutions.

Topics suited for this model: Community issues such as racism, violence, regional sprawl, and more. Any issue for which community members need to be part of crafting a solution.

Future Search is a unique planning method used by communities and organizations to enable large, diverse groups to validate a common mission, take responsibility for action, and develop commitment to implementation. The meeting is task-focused. It brings people from all walks of life into the same conversation—those with resources, expertise, formal authority, and need. People tell stories about their past, present, and desired future. Through dialogue they discover their common ground and then they make concrete action plans.

The meeting design comes from theories and principles tested in many cultures for the past fifty years. It relies on mutual learning among stakeholders as a catalyst for voluntary action and follow-up. People devise new forms of cooperation that continue for months or years.

Use Future Search when: It is important that everyone have the same large picture in order to act responsibly. The method is especially useful in uncertain, fast-changing situations.

Topics suited for this model: Housing, employment, transportation, education, and more.

The Harwood Institute for Public Innovation's Turning Outward practice is a step-by-step process intended to encourage leaders to use the community, rather than a conference room, as the reference point for choices and judgments. Turning Outward entails taking steps to better understand communities; changing processes and thinking to make conversations more community-focused; being proactive on community issues; and putting community aspirations first.

The Turning Outward approach involves asking the right questions to find out what your community really wants and bringing together the right teams to help make those dreams a reality.

Use Turning Outward when: You want to identify and learn more about your community's needs and desires. Libraries around the country are using the approach to better understand their communities and to bring about positive change.

Topics suited for this model: Any conversation in which community members are tasked with exploring their aspirations, concerns, and the steps it might take to achieve those aspirations. This approach can apply to a variety of topics.

National Issues Forums offer citizens the opportunity to come together to deliberate, to make choices with others about ways to approach difficult issues, and to work toward creating reasoned public judgment. National Issues Forums are known for careful issue framing and quality issue guides, which outline three or four different viewpoints.

Forums are neutrally moderated in a way that encourages positive interaction between people who are not expected to agree but are encouraged to find a shared direction. For two or three hours, participants are led by a neutral moderator who encourages exploration and evaluation of several possible solutions to the issue at hand. Every solution comes with a set of costs and consequences that must be thoroughly measured. Only then do you know which costs participants are willing to bear.

Use National Issues Forums when: You want to encourage exploration of tough public problems to increase public knowledge of the issue, or you wish to influence public decisions and policy.

Topics suited for this model: Health care, immigration, policing, substance abuse, energy, climate change, and more! National Issues Forums provide materials on a variety of topics, including historical frameworks for reflecting on big issues in history.

World Cafés enable groups of people to participate in evolving rounds of dialogue while remaining part of a single, larger, connected conversation. Small, intimate conversations link to and build on each other as people move between groups, cross-pollinate ideas, and discover new insights into questions or issues that really matter in their life, work, or community. World Café–style conversations are a creative process for leading collaborative dialogue, sharing knowledge, and creating possibilities for action in groups of all sizes.

In a World Café event, participants sit four or five to a table and have a series of conversational rounds about a question that is personally meaningful to them.

After several rounds, each table reports its themes, insights, and learning to the whole group. That information is captured on flip charts or other means for making it visible, allowing everyone to reflect on what is emerging in the room.

Use World Café when: You want to encourage exploration of a topic or of participants' own views and experiences as well as the experiences of others or to explore and develop innovative ideas and solutions.

Topics suited for this model: A whole range of topics can be adapted to a World Café process. You can explore topics important to your community, such as immigration and community-building, religion, planning issues, land use, and more.

CONTRIBUTORS

AUDREY BARBAKOFF is the community engagement and economic development manager at King County Library System in Washington State. She is the author of *Adults Just Wanna Have Fun: Programs for Emerging Adults* (ALA Editions, 2016). She writes, speaks, and teaches nationally on innovative adult programs, services, and community engagement. Audrey is a *Library Journal* Mover and Shaker and was recognized by the *Kitsap Peninsula Business Journal*'s 40 Under 40 award program. She holds an MLIS from the University of Washington and is pursuing her EdD from the University of Southern California, where she is researching capacity building for community-led planning in libraries. Find her at www.the-bookaneer.com.

QUANETTA "Q" BATTS is the director for outreach and engagement at The Ohio State University Libraries. She provides leadership and cultivates relationships with campus and community partners. Q also manages the OSU Libraries' Mary P. Key Diversity Residency Program, the Expanding Visions Foundation internship program, and Project Mentor with Big Brothers Big Sisters. She is an exceptional project manager who leads conference planning and strategic projects. Q is also an experienced workshop presenter, covering topics such as negotiation strategies and event management. In April 2019 Q was recognized with the university's Distinguished Staff Award. She has an MBA and a BS from Ohio Dominican University.

ANDREA BLACKMAN currently serves as the division director for the Nashville Public Library's Civil Rights Center, Special Collections Center, and Votes for Women Center; she also is an adjunct professor at Lipscomb University and Vanderbilt University's Peabody College. Her ongoing research includes education disparity and self-representations in children's literature; anti-racism, racism, and racial inequality; African Diaspora; the modern civil rights movement; Caribbean history and literature; oral history methodologies; and community engagement and equity. At the Nashville Public Library, Blackman advocates for professional leadership, equitable accountability, and cultural engagement.

HADIYA EVANS is a reference and adult programming librarian at the Rodolfo "Corky" Gonzales Branch of the Denver Public Library, holding an MA and an MLIS in Library Information. Her professional trajectory has been not a sprint but a marathon, with pit stops that have enriched her career through the inspiration and guidance of unofficial mentorship. Hadiya's strong commitment to engagement is rooted in nurturing collaborative partnerships and creating relevant and community-focused programming. She is vice president of the newly formed Colorado Black Library Association, an affiliate of the Black Caucus of the American Library Association.

Helping organizations see the big picture as they strive for equity and social justice is **CINDY FESEMYER'S** passion. She is the adult and community services consultant for the state library team at the Wisconsin Department of Public Instruction. Previously she served seven years as director of the Columbus (Wisconsin) Public Library, named a finalist for *Library Journal's* 2017 Best Small Library in America. She sits on the board of the Public Library Association and is a trustee for the Madison Public Library. Librarianship is Cindy's second career. After fourteen years of managing nonprofits, she earned her MLIS from the University of Wisconsin–Madison in 2012.

ERICA FREUDENBERGER has been creating community-led change for decades. Currently the outreach and engagement consultant at the Southern Adirondack Library System, she formerly led Red Hook Public Library, a finalist for *Library Journal's* Best Small Library in America award. She took part in the *Re-envisioning Public Libraries* pilot with the Aspen Institute. In 2014 she took part in the American Library Association's Libraries Transforming Communities initiative. Named a 2016 *Library Journal* Mover and Shaker in the category of Community Builder, she also garnered the Public Library Association's Upstart Innovation Award in 2019. She founded Thriving Libraries, LLC to help libraries create sustainable, resilient communities.

TASNEEM ANSARIYAH GRACE is a performance artist who facilitates engagements that explore the soul connection of our collective humanity. For nearly twenty years she worked as a newspaper journalist and has worked with several nonprofits in Syracuse, New York; Nashville, Tennessee; and Belize in Central America as a community engagement manager, content creator, and editor. Currently, she serves at the Nashville Public Library as an associate director of programming in the Civil Rights Center. As a student and teacher of the global struggles for liberation, she continues to use conversation and stories as a pathway to developing community.

SUSAN HILDRETH is a library consultant in Walnut Creek, California. She recently served as treasurer for the American Library Association and was a fellow with the Aspen Institute's Dialogue on Public Libraries. She was the Distinguished Practitioner in Residence at the University of Washington iSchool and led the Institute of Museum and Library Services from 2011 through 2015. Hildreth has held library leadership positions including California state librarian and city librarian for the Seattle and San Francisco Public Libraries. She has a BA from Syracuse University, an MLS from the State University of New York at Albany, and an MBA from Rutgers University.

ELLEN M. KNUTSON is a Portland, Oregon–based research associate at the Charles F. Kettering Foundation, where she is a key member of the team learning from U.S. and Russian librarians who are creating community-focused libraries. She is an adjunct assistant professor at the School of Information Sciences at the University of Illinois. Knutson also serves on the advisory committee for the American Library Association's Center for Civic Life. She received her MS and PhD in library and information science from the University of Illinois at Urbana-Champaign and a BA in political science from Reed College.

NANCY KRANICH teaches at Rutgers University and works on special projects with its libraries. After service as president of the American Library Association, Kranich founded ALA's Center for Civic Life and the Libraries Foster Community Engagement Member Initiative Group. Trained as a public innovator with the Harwood Institute for Public Innovation, she also serves on the board of the National Issues Forums Institute and co-leads the U.S.-Russia Dialogue on the Civic Role of Libraries in the 21st Century. She earned an MPA from New York University and an MA in library science and a BA in anthropology from the University of Wisconsin–Madison.

NANCY KIM PHILLIPS is the community engagement manager at Skokie Public Library, where she leads a team of staff and volunteers who respond to community interests and needs in collaboration with partner organizations. These efforts include a wide range of programs, services, and collective impact projects concerning early childhood development, school services, economic development, health, immigrant services, accessibility, healthy aging, civic engagement, neighborhood engagement, and equity. Before undertaking librarianship, Nancy worked extensively with nonprofit organizations in the areas of collaboration and strategic planning.

SARAH GOODWIN THIEL is the faculty and community engagement librarian for the University of Kansas (KU) Libraries. She holds an MA in library science from the University of Missouri and a BA with a specialization in studio art/printmaking from Southern Illinois University. Thiel is the coordinator of the Haricombe Gallery Exhibits Program and oversees the development and installation of campuswide collaborative, transdisciplinary exhibitions. She works to foster an environment of engagement within KU Libraries and to cultivate relationships with the wider community. Thiel presents regularly on topics relating to engagement, collaboration, and improved access to scholarship, collections, and resources.

AMBER WILLIAMS has worked in public libraries for more than a decade in Washington State. Her community engagement work earned her recognition from *Library Journal* as a 2019 Mover and Shaker and an Advances in Library Services Award from the Washington Library Association (WLA) in 2017. To help keep a broad view of library work, she currently serves as an American Library Association Council member-at-large and is a past WLA chair of the Public Library Division. Amber is committed to shifting library culture to one of engagement. Her latest project includes working with libraries in the Wisconsin Libraries Transforming Communities initiative.

INDEX

CPSIA information can be obtained
at www.ICGtesting.com
Printed in the USA
LVHW100817290921
698963LV00002B/4

You may also be interested in

ISBN: 978-0-8389-4799-9

ISBN: 978-0-8389-4811-8

ISBN: 978-0-8389-4739-5

ISBN: 978-0-8389-4631-2

ISBN: 978-0-8389-1981-1

ISBN: 978-0-8389-4974-0

alastore.ala.org

ALA Editions

American Library Association
225 N. Michigan Ave., Suite 1300
Chicago, IL 60601-7616

1 (866) SHOPALA   (866) 746-7252
www.alastore.ala.org

ISBN 978-0-8389-4740-1

9 780838 947401